In a rut?

Going nowhere?

Frustrated with life?

WHAT'S HOLDING YOU BACK?

Would you like to know?

Bernard H. Burgess

Grateful acknowledgement is made to the following for permissions to quote: Whitaker House, 30 Hunt Valley Circle, New Kensington, PA 15068, for *Maximized Manhood,* copyright 1982 by Edwin Louis Cole; Bantam Books Inc, a division of Bantam, Doubleday, Dell Publishing Group, Inc., 1540 Broadway, New York, NY 10036, for *University of Success,* copyright 1982 by Og Mandino; Ballantine Books, 201 E. 50th St., New York, NY 10022, for *The Master Key To Riches,* copyright 1965 by Napoleon Hill; and Prentice Hall, Simon & Schuster, Inc., 240 Frisch Court, Paramus, NJ 07652, for *The Magic of Thinking Big,* copyright 1959 by David J. Schwartz.

Published by Success Concepts

ISBN 0-9664764-0-9

Library of Congress Catalog Card Number: 98-90352

Manufactured in the United States of America

Cover design by Seth Meierotto of
Yellowstone Printing & Design

DEDICATION

I wish to dedicate this book to the most important people in my life. First, to my wife, Olivia, for her years of standing by me, even when there didn't seem like a lot of good reasons to do so. Secondly, to my parents, Bernard and Ruth Burgess, for their loving and caring examples of the best qualities in mankind. Lastly, I dedicate this effort to our future... our children. To my daughter, Heidi, and to my grandchildren, Chance and Hailey, I hope this may help bring prosperity to your lives in exchange for the joy you've brought to mine.

ACKNOWLEDGEMENTS

I wish to thank the following people for their time and patience in reviewing my various chapters and for their suggestions and feedback, without which I would have been seriously hampered. First and foremost, I thank my wife, Olivia, for her support in all aspects of creating this book. She has been my greatest reviewer, critic, and promoter, and I could not have done this without her! Numerous other people read and provided feedback, but none so much as Monte Crummer, and his inputs were extremely valuable. Others who also assisted in various ways were Ed Riley, Father Joe Daley, Francis Dubs, Mary Charles Capps, Tina Wilson, and Tim Carver.

TABLE OF CONTENTS

FORWARD

Have you ever felt like your life just isn't as good as it ought to be? Do you feel like you're "stuck in a rut," and not sure how to get out of it? Are your dreams gathering dust in the back room of your mind, more like empty promises rather than hopeful possibilities? Is life not as interesting, satisfying, exciting, and fulfilling as you had wanted it to be? If your answer is "yes," do you know why you feel as you do? Do you know what's holding you back?

When I left an Air Force career and re-entered the civilian world, I thought I knew what to expect. However, my expectations did not match the reality that I found. One of my goals has been to talk to and get to know many people in the numerous places we've lived. Instead of the sense of optimism, hope, and ambition I anticipated, I found a widespread lethargy, frustration, and lack of motivation permeating the social fabric of this country. As I explored the minds and attitudes of more and more good men and women, I started to develop a growing sense of the things that were going wrong for myself, and for them. There were recognizable thought habits and tendencies which seemed to affect most of us to varying degrees.

The more I observed these common thought habits, the more I wanted to understand them. I began to study the works of many of our best known authors on relationships, achievement, and success. It became apparent that if I could go through more than forty years of life, a master's degree in formal education, and a professional career, yet still be grossly ignorant of key success principles... perhaps there were many others in the same situation. While there are many outstanding books and other resources which show us what to do to improve our lives, I have never ran across one which first explained how we're short-circuiting our own goals and dreams. For me, at least, I needed to understand what I was doing wrong and how it was hurting me, before I knew what to try to change. That has been the motivation behind this book!

1

It is my hope that this will be a valuable resource for those of you who want to dig into the recesses of your mind and figure out what you may be doing to keep life from giving you what you want.

There are many aspects of success. We all either know or have heard about the "poor little rich boy," who, despite his wealth, is miserable. From this, we can surmise that there is more to life than just money and material wealth. In fact, the real wealth of life involves far more than just our finances. To be truly wealthy and successful, a person must also have harmonious and worthwhile relationships, hope for a better future, faith, good health, a satisfying job or occupation, a mind which is open and eager to learn, a caring and giving nature, freedom from fear and torment, contentment with one's position in life, and love. Financial and material status is only one of the ways we measure success and achievement... perhaps it is even the least important. However, in a free enterprise economic system, a person cannot be totally successful nor free unless they are also successful financially!

In 1998 America, despite the relatively resurgent economy, most people still list lack of money and an inability to get ahead as pressing problems. For the typical individual and family, if money is lacking, many other qualities are probably inadequate as well. Money problems create stresses which affect and limit other areas of our lives. For these reasons, this book may seem more related to financial matters, than to other areas. This stems from two beliefs. One, the vast majority of readers can relate to financial improvement. Two, *the factors and concepts to be discussed are as important to all other qualities of life, as they are to financial growth and success.* Regardless of the achievement yardstick we use, financial or otherwise, the obstacles which hold us back, and the principles for going forward, are essentially the same.

In this book, I use examples from forty years of life experiences, mostly as an Air Force officer and businessperson, to help the reader relate to individual concepts. Many examples relate to my own experiences, but most are composites of numerous people I have known and worked with. Some readers may feel I am talking about you, personally, or may be uncomfortable with selected topics. If so, that's good, because it means I'm relating to you, perhaps in areas which are keeping you from reaching your full potential. Large numbers of people are in similar positions and have the same mental hang-ups that you and I do. You, and those things which hold you back, are not unique, in this context!

Many books tell us that we're all OK. This is not one of them! From my experience, people need to know and face the hard realities, before they will find the courage and inner strength to do something about the obstacles in their lives. *Nobody can help us achieve fuller and more rewarding lives unless we first honestly look inside ourselves.* When I truly began to strive for growth, improvement, and positive change in my life, I did not feel very comfortable with, nor did I sometimes even like, the person I saw in the mirror. Keep in mind that it is your choice, alone, whether or not to look in the mirror!

If you are married, or have a significant other, I would suggest that you explore these pages together. Working together as a team, we can accomplish far more, faster, than we will as an individual. In addition, these thought processes are somewhat universal, and probably affect your partner in some ways too. At the very least, your partner should be aware of your mind exploration and development, so they can understand and support your changes. A sure way to encounter resistance or failure is to try to change yourself without taking the time and effort to educate and involve your chosen mate. Our mate is our equal, they should also be an equal and involved partner in our growth and development.

This book focuses on identifying and understanding the thought habits which most hinder our progress and success potential. It offers techniques and suggestions for overcoming each, but the focus is not on solutions. *Once a reader recognizes a possible problem, a bibliography of suggested resources can help them begin to deal with it.* Chapter One is a negative, and perhaps even depressing, observation of how mediocrity is affecting our country and our lives. Don't despair, though, for the second chapter makes the case for the continual pursuit of excellence, and should challenge you to live your life to the fullest. The third, and subsequent, chapters each deal with specific attitudes or thought processes which prevent us from living more rewarding lives. You will possibly relate to some, and, if you feel like you're *"stuck in a rut,"* you might find.... ***"what's holding you back?"***

"It isn't that they can't see the solution. It is that they can't see the problem." (G. K. Chesterton)

HOW TO USE THIS BOOK MOST EFFECTIVELY:

A. Note those chapters dealing with areas which may be holding you back:

_____

_____

_____

_____

B. List those recommended books and other resources you intend to use:

_____

_____

_____

_____

_____

C. State your top 5 goals from reading this book:
1.
_____

2.
_____

3.
_____

4.
_____

5.
_____

D. Write clearly what your definite major purpose is (be very specific):

_____

_____

_____

_____

E. What is your self-improvement plan as it relates to your definite major purpose and your top 5 goals, established above:

_____

_____

_____

_____

F. Notes:

_____

_____

_____

CHAPTER ONE
MEDIOCRITY!!.... A NATIONAL ADDICTION?

In the earth's most prosperous nation, the United States, having vast resources and opportunities, the great majority of men and women live lives of mediocrity, or worse, often impoverished in their finances, personal development, relationships, and spirit! Many successful executives and professionals achieve high incomes, yet have poor marriages, no time freedom, and high stress which often erodes their health and shortens their lives. Men, women and children risk their lives to come to this country in rafts which barely float, with little more than the clothes they wear, and become national academic champions, successful businesspeople, doctors, attorneys, prosperous, wealthy, even happy. Meanwhile, most native citizens go through life accomplishing little, just 'getting by' or 'existing'! What's keeping us from achieving our full potential? History may provide some insight.

When the first pioneers arrived several centuries ago, they found a virgin and untamed land of great natural resources, and virtually unlimited opportunity. With no existing industries, these hardy settlers were on their own. Most cleared the land and established farms, and many started their own businesses. Thus, this nation began with independent, predominantly self-employed, free-enterprisers. The limited demand for employment and employees often served more as a stepping stone to learning a trade or craft so one could go off on his own. Lifetime employment was virtually unheard of.

One hundred years later, we find that the majority of people were still in various cottage industries and farming. At the turn of the twentieth century, we were still an agricultural nation. However, a major shift was beginning to occur in how Americans earned their livings.

As we entered the industrial age, large corporations evolved to produce the materials and products of an increasingly complex society. Large businesses need employees to mass produce the weapons, tools, and toys of a rapidly growing nation. So began the industrial age, and so began the breakneck transition from a nation of small businesspeople... to a nation of employees!

The United States, in a few short decades, transitioned to an urban society, as our citizenry raced from the farms to the cities to capture the lucrative jobs in corporate America. Major institutions shifted their operations and teachings to support and promote this trend. Schools oriented their curriculums to accommodate and teach future employees, rather than future business men and women. Our families, to some extent our churches, and certainly our governments, hopped on the 'lifetime employment' bandwagon. In a few decades, society was oriented to support, promote and teach 'job-ism.' Little incentive existed to promote and teach business and self-employment. Our transition into the Industrial Age was complete.

Today, the Industrial era is giving way to the Communications Age. Benefitted by the telephone, television, radio, fax, computer, cellular and satellite technologies, and the availability of national and international travel, the business world has become global in scope. Gone are the days when a large business could limit itself to a local or even a national perspective. Both the market and the competition are becoming international, for most companies. This demands that corporations carefully control costs, the largest usually being employee payroll and benefits.

Once-sacred benefits, such as insurance and retirement packages, are frequently sacrificed to 'bottom line profit' and to 'stockholder dividends.' The modern-day employee cannot expect to work a full career with any one company, but will change jobs or occupations several times in his working life. Downsizing, rightsizing, outsourcing, layoffs, buyouts, and foreign production are among the current trends resulting in job insecurity and pay stagnation. Combined with the always increasing cost of living, the average person's buying power and real standard of living has declined, for the past two decades!

The economic reality in the 1990's is that both spouses are usually employed in most families. Yet, most households spend virtually all their incomes just to maintain an acceptable standard of living, leaving little or none for savings, education, medical emergencies, or retirement. Federal and state taxes take 45% of the average family income. Lifestyle is often financed by debt, and every man, woman and child averages more than $5000 in high interest credit card obligations. With most of the work force dependent upon employment, their choices are limited and future often uncertain, caught between stagnant wages, periods of unemployment, and steadily rising costs. The end result is that most people reaching age 65 are unable to live with financial dignity; often unable to live without family or government assistance, or continuing to work!

As the average citizen becomes less able to meet their financial needs, federal and state governments are expected to provide more services. Federal 'Social Welfare' expenditures were 57 % of the yearly budget in 1995; triple that spent on national defense. Nearly ten percent of the US population (about 25 million people) receives food stamps. Fourteen percent of our population cannot afford health insurance, and Medicare and Medicaid must often pick up the tab. The Department of Health and Human Services reported that, in 1990, over one-trillion dollars was spent on total public welfare. This amounts to 19.1% of the Gross Domestic Product! The burden upon government is becoming unbearable: in 1998, the federal debt is approaching six-trillion dollars, with little expectation of serious reduction. The National League of Cities estimates that literally half of all US towns and cities are broke! Intense debate rages about how to keep the Social Security Trust Fund solvent, as the Board of Trustees estimates the current program will be unable to pay full benefits by the year 2029. The same Trustees report that the Health Insurance Trust Fund, which funds Medicare, faces total depletion by the year 2001, without major legislative changes. Federal and state governments grapple with plans to reduce the welfare rolls and welfare dependency. Meanwhile, individuals and families face their own personal challenges.

Money Magazine just reported the results of a national survey showing that three out of five Americans worry often about money, even thinking about it more than they do sex! The Social Security Administration reports that fourteen percent of all Americans (36.5 million) live below the poverty income level: $16,036 per year in 1996. The federal government estimates that over three million citizens are homeless, and over twenty percent of all children live in poverty. Fourteen million children reportedly received over $22 billion in Aid for Families with Dependent Children in 1992. The Census Bureau's most recent report shows that incomes rose 1.2% in 1996; however, adjusted for inflation, the typical household income is still 2.7% less than in 1989. Over 75% of us earn less than $25,000 per year. Only 6% have incomes exceeding $50,000 yearly. Despite our current six year economic expansion, the average family has less spending power today, than it did eight years ago!

As parents work harder to make up for decreasing real income, the time devoted to family decreases. The average father gives his children less than 1 minute of undivided attention, per day! The Nebraska Attorney General, in a 1996 newspaper article entitled *A Nation Awash In Television*, reported that the typical child watches over 25 hours of television per week, more time than is spent in religious services, talking to parents, reading, or even listening to teachers. In his 1982 book, *Maximized Manhood*, Edwin Louis Cole devotes a chapter to the Video Daddy, and states, "The greatest addiction in America is not marijuana, cocaine, or pills. It is television." A 1995 poll by the Family Research Council shows that 90% of Americans believe the media affects violent crime. Is it surprising that our children are more influenced by TV and computers, than by their own parents?

Divorce has become the solution of choice to resolve marital issues! More than half of first and second-time marriages fail. Lack of money is cited as a major contributing factor by most of those surveyed. The emotional toll is heavy on both spouses and children. Nearly four of every ten US children live in fatherless households. More than one-third of all children under the age of six live without Dad at home.

The Census Bureau reports that 30% of all US births are to unwed mothers. Every day, 3000 teenage, unwed girls become pregnant, contributing to over one-and-a-half-million abortions performed in this nation, yearly. Schools must provide programs for 'latch-key kids,' whose parents are unavailable outside of school hours. Child Care is a rapidly growing industry. With less parental supervision and involvement, we have an epidemic of youth suicides, runaways, street gangs, drug use and crime, often by violent child predators. Every hour of every day in the US: 50 teenage girls give birth; 120 children run away from home; 60 children are abused; two are killed by guns; two are arrested for drunk driving; and 500 are arrested for a drug-related offense.

The child advocacy program, America's Promise, headed by retired General Colin Powell, in January 1998, reported on the condition of America's children. They estimate that there are over 14 million "at-risk" children in the United States. Of these, 4 million are members of street gangs. They also report that youth crime increases by 300 percent just during the one hour immediately following school.

Martin Luther King said: "To ignore evil is to become an accomplice to it." Sadly, the good people of this nation are too often ignoring the needs of our children. It is not difficult to see who is, and who is not, raising America's children. Day care workers, babysitters, television, movie producers, video arcades, computers, gangs, and peer pressure are molding and teaching our future leaders...our sons and daughters. Not Dad and Mom!

A major underlying cause of our problems is a national attitude which accepts mediocrity! We suffer from a mental laziness which shows up in declining educational standards and test scores, often among the lowest within the industrialized nations. Under the influence of John Dewey, educational curriculums were re-oriented to concentrate on social behavior over traditional teaching of the basics. This has led to the educational movements toward pass/fail and other measurement standards which downplay excellence and focus instead upon the average. In February 1998, US students competed against those of 20 other industrial nations in math and science testing. Our youngsters finished in 18th place, bettering only three other nations' scholars! When President Clinton was asked why, his reply was "There is no excuse!"

America's Promise spokesman, General Colin Powell, says that fully one-half of America's youth cannot read up to their age and grade level. In June 1997, the USA Today newspaper reported that, in California alone, 53% of high school graduates who went on to college required tutoring in the basics due to deficiencies in public schooling. The Department of Education estimates that about 20% of our population are "functionally illiterate," unable to function in a complex society, and another 34% are only "marginally literate"! They also report that our high school dropout rate is 27% (compared to 2% in the former Soviet Union!). The United Nations recently ranked the United States 49th in literacy rate among more than 150 member nations (this is a drop of 18 places since 1950!).

The attitude of mediocrity is apparent among our chronic unemployed, generations of welfare families, as well as educational dropouts. It is the catalyst behind the explosive growth in social service programs, counseling services, and our prison system. Government lotteries and gambling casinos respond to our widespread something-for-nothing and get-rich-quick ethic. We continue to rely too-heavily upon the perceived security and lower responsibility of jobs, rather than accepting the challenges and risks of business-ownership. In his 1995 book, *You Can't Steal Second With Your Foot on First,*

Burke Hedges asks the sobering question: "...is Job-ism a bigger threat to America than Communism?"

In modern day America the vast majority of our work force continues to work for someone else, despite the fact that very few are truly succeeding as a result. Is it a coincidence that, according to government statistics, less than five percent of us will ever see a day of financial independence in retirement? We, as citizens, seem committed to the path of least resistance... mediocrity... rather than embracing change, challenge, and excellence!

My hometown newspaper editorialized last year about a group of community leaders visiting from one of the former Soviet republics. They observed Americans to have an almost "sheep-like conformity." Instead of the nation of free thinkers and independent, action-oriented people they expected to find, they perceived us to be lethargic, unmotivated, and almost totally dependent upon following the herd! (One only has to watch the miles and miles of taillights, during any morning and evening rush hour, to understand their perception). This is a particularly disturbing observation coming from people accustomed to the stagnation of communism.

In his 1982 book, *University of Success*, Og Mandino introduces lesson 33 with these words:

...Why do so many of us act as if we were sheep? Why do we abandon the management of our lives to others while we stumble forlornly through each day waiting only for the next command to jump or bow or perform for our supper? Whenever we allow others to control our lives we place our future in their hands, we abdicate our right to make choices beneficial to us, and we stifle all opportunity for growth. With no goals, no priorities, no life strategy of our own, we drift with the herd through an endless meadow of mediocrity, unable to break loose, to achieve even a small part of the dreams we once cherished....

CHAPTER TWO
DEMANDING OUR BEST?
(THE CASE FOR "EXCELLENCE")

Do you and I, as human beings, parents, US citizens, world citizens... have an obligation to be the very best we are capable of being? Or, do we have the right to fall short? Well short?

In chapter one we looked at the trends toward mediocrity, which plague our nation. Subsequent chapters will explore the specific characteristics which hold us back. Now, we will consider the reasons for pursuing excellence.

Do you remember the dreams you had as a child, the imaginary games you played, the characters you became? It seemed possible to become anything you wanted to be. Failure, or being second best, was not on your mind. You just expected life to give you what you wished.

As you matured, you probably felt a sense of pride during key events in your life: grade school graduation, high school entry, honor roll, high school graduation, college, college graduation, marriage, the birth of your child. You likely felt invincible and in control of your life; that the whole world was your oyster; that all life's options were available to you. Didn't you expect to conquer the world and succeed at whatever you decided to do?

Life has a way of dulling our dreams, especially if challenges and obstacles have slowed or stopped us. Despite your challenges, though, don't you still secretly want to be 'somebody'? Don't you still dream of being a hero, doctor, politician, astronaut; of being famous or wealthy, traveling the world, eating at the nicest restaurants, staying in the best resorts, giving to your favorite causes? Are you truly content being less than you thought you'd be; having less than you want to have; doing less than you are capable of doing? Doesn't your inner voice tell you that you deserve more, regardless of the past?

Search your innermost feelings. Don't you expect the **most** from your life, not the least? Time and events may postpone and deaden our dreams, may make us reluctant to even think about them, but the dreams are still buried in our subconscious. We're born believing we can become 'somebody,' that we have a potential to reach, and circumstances may obscure but cannot kill that belief. **In each of us, I believe there burns a desire for excellence.**

Those family members who care about us want the best for us and the best from us. Your parents probably told you that you can do anything, that you can succeed if you really try, that you can become who you want to be, and they believe in you. Those who said such things sincerely expressed the potential they saw in you; their genuine desire for your success.

If you are a parent, yourself, you look at your son or daughter and see not just the child but also the potential. Dad sees himself playing ball with his son (maybe his daughter, too), hunting or fishing. Mom sees the good friends they'll become, the things they'll do together, how proud she'll be as her child grows and blossoms. We all share dreams of our sons or daughters achieving things in life that we never thought possible. We love our children, and for that reason we want them to reach their maximum potential and have the best that life offers. No good parent would want or expect less. If we expect the best of our children, doesn't it make sense that our parents and family expect only the best from us?

As parents, we automatically assume leadership positions within our homes. From birth, until well after they've grown and moved out, we are a leader, an example, and a role model for our children... whether we like it or not, whether we accept it or not, and whether we do it right or not. Children first look to Mom and Dad for guidance, ahead of all others. We owe it to our children to set an example of excellence, in all that we do, in all that we are! Webster's Dictionary defines hypocrisy as "pretending to be what one is not, or to feel what one does not, especially a pretense of virtue...." If you and I teach and encourage our children to be the best, to always do their very best; while we live only lives of mediocrity, falling far short of our potential... we are hypocrites! It cannot be rationalized any other way. If we love our children, and want only the best of them and for them, you and I must willingly set the example of excellence in all areas of our lives. Anything less, is hypocrisy.

In your job, occupation or profession, second-rate performance is unacceptable. Your boss has never told you to lower your standards. If you own a business, you would never tell your employees to do sloppy work. Regardless of the occupation, job or profession, we are expected to do our best. The ditchdigger keeps his job by digging ditches better than anyone else who wants his job. The doctor builds his practice and stays in business by being excellent at what he does. The business owner must satisfy the customer, who wants the best value for his money. In virtually every job a person may do, every product you may make, every service one may perform, someone expects our best effort. Only 'excellence' can insure continued demand for your skills, product or service; staying in business; keeping your job; reaching your dreams!

Can a democracy, or our great Republic, last without strong citizens committed to excellence in all that they do? Do we have a moral responsibility to be the best citizens we are capable of being? Or, are we so strong as a nation that we can, individually, be mediocre?

History shows that great nations rise and fall, like the tides. We can observe a pattern to the rise and fall of a nation, just as there is a predictable pattern to the life and death of a person. Since nations are people, their collective attitudes drive the stages in their nation's lifespan. The attitudes which build a great nation stem from a pioneering spirit and the desire for a better life; for qualities, such as **freedom**, for which there is no substitute. Our recorded history indicates that stagnation and decline are also related to collective attitudes.

Japan, for example, fell to defeat following an attitude of

aggression leading to World War II. Following defeat, Japan's mediocrity was best represented by the phrase 'made in Japan,' which conjured images of cheap stir sticks for drinks. However, over the past two decades, as the Japanese vision and attitude changed to one of confidence, boldness, and excellence, the same phrase became synonymous with high quality and value.

The old Soviet Union experienced national decay due to decades of personal insignificance under the Communist system. Communism destroyed their will to achieve anything other than mediocrity! With no incentives for profit, for land ownership, for recognition, for personal growth, the average citizen became lethargic, indifferent, and unmotivated to do and be anything more than the minimum. Alcoholism became a widespread addiction. With a weak moral standard, leadership became corrupt and self-serving. Communism has become synonymous with sloppy workmanship, environmental devastation, mental and moral bankruptcy, and national deterioration. As we plunge further and further into Socialism, is the same thing happening to us?

We could probably relate the decline and fall of nearly all nations to an increasingly immoral or mediocre national will, and if true, then we must ask if the same is true for the United States (and other free nations). Is a nation, like a chain, only as strong as its weakest link? Regardless of our military might, our abundant resources, our land and waterways... **is citizenship becoming our 'weak link'?** The trends referenced in chapter one certainly suggest this possibility. If so, we could doom our nation to chronic and widespread decline as an inevitable result of the societal trends toward mediocrity... unless we reverse these trends!

Democracies and republics are based upon the principle that the individual has worth and value, that each has inalienable rights and responsibilities. If government is truly "of the people, by the people, and for the people," then the people must be able to lead as well as be lead. In an ever-changing world, facing new frontiers and challenges, our citizenry will be capable of national and international leadership only if we are constantly growing, developing and evolving: in attitude, knowledge, mental toughness, human kindness, moral fiber and resolve. The instant we allow mediocrity to gain momentum within our citizenry... is the instant we begin to erode our freedoms and risk our way of life! If we look deeply and honestly at ourselves, we are already at risk!

The truth must be, that every individual citizen in this great nation has a moral responsibility to themselves, their children, other citizens, our nation, and to our founding fathers and mothers, to constantly expand and refine our skills and capabilities as a person, citizen, and leader. If we fail to meet our responsibilities, we are not a fully productive citizen. At worst, our failure will contribute to trends toward lower standards and the growth of socialism in America!

American Presidents, and other leaders, consistently challenge us to do our best and be our best. This is nowhere more evident than during the inaugural addresses. None sums it up better and more succinctly than John F. Kennedy, when he said "Ask not what your country can do for you. Ask what you can do for your country." It is obvious that a nation must have strong citizens, to be strong itself. Individual strength is created by continuously accepting the challenge, growth, change, commitment, principles and excellence which forged this nation.

If citizenship requires us to be the best we are capable of being, does our religious faith also demand excellence of us? In Christianity, the Bible has many references which challenge us to achieve and excel in our lives, not just drift through accomplishing little. In Matthew 25, the Parable of the Talents, Jesus tells of a prosperous traveler who must leave his home and business for an extended period. The traveler leaves a portion of his wealth, measured in "talents," in the safekeeping of three of his servants. One is given five talents to safeguard, another two, and the last receives one. Upon the master's return, the first servant gives back the five talents plus five more he has earned from wisely investing and managing the master's money. For his loyalty, honesty and efficiency, the servant is rewarded with greatly increased responsibility and resources!

The second servant also wisely used the two talents he was entrusted with, and presents the master with double his money: four talents. This servant, as well, is praised and rewarded with significantly expanded pay and responsibility. The third servant, however, had essentially buried his one talent in the backyard, had not increased its value at all, and returns the original talent to his boss. Expecting praise and reward for maintaining the original talent, and not losing it, the servant is instead harshly scolded. He is even called a "wicked and slothful servant" for not showing the ambition and character to see that his entrusted talent increased in value. The message is clear that we are expected to use our given "talents" to their greatest purpose and value; anything less makes us undeserving to retain stewardship of even those blessings we had!

In the Christian faith, we are called upon, by our Bible and our churches, to give to those less fortunate than ourselves. However, before we can give to someone else, we must have something to give! Those who have little or nothing, can only give little or nothing. Those who spend all their time just making a living, don't even have time to volunteer. Even the glorious Mother Theresa, laid to rest with international recognition and praise, was limited in what she could accomplish without financial contributions and volunteers. There can be no 'charity,' without 'prosperity'! If we're all beggars, who are we going to beg from?

The Bible tells us how to live. The third epistle of John, verse two, says (paraphrased): I wish above all things that you may prosper and be in health, even as your soul prospers. Jesus tells us, in Matthew 12:35, that a good man out of the good treasure of the heart brings forth good things. In Proverbs 13:22, we're told that a good man leaves an inheritance to his children's children. We are not told to be poor, nor mediocre. We are told to "prosper," to be "good," to acquire an "inheritance" worthy to leave our grandchildren! If we are true to our faith, how can we tolerate doing, being, having, giving, caring... less than the **best** of which we are capable?

We are blessed with the greatest potential of any creature on this planet! Our bodies are capable of a tremendous variety of complex skills. Surgeons can perform extremely delicate operations. Athletes run faster, jump farther, and lift more with every passing year. Our brains are the most complex on earth! Nobody knows our full potential, because no person can measure it, let alone achieve it. The physically handicapped show us the awesome power of the brain to overcome staggering odds. People inspire us with their mental toughness and attitude, their determination to think their way to worthy achievement despite their challenges. Around the globe, we see evidence of man's ability to reason, learn, search, evaluate, experiment, and combine matter and energy into monumental design and function. You and I have the same capacity for success. Why would we have such great potential... and not strive to achieve it?

Princess Diana, of Wales, with her tragic death, stirred the hearts and souls of people the world over. Was it just because she was a princess? No. She moved us, in life and in death, because we admired her passion for life, her struggle to overcome hardships and heartbreaks, her drive to do things that were worthy of being done. We related to Diana because she had the ambition and fighting spirit to live life on her terms, not someone else's. Don't we all wish we had that?

Diana's early death reminded us that life is uncertain, precious, and all-too-short! The "candle in the wind" can burn brightly one minute and be extinguished the next. Neither you nor I know which heartbeat will be our last. All the things we are planning to do 'tomorrow,' or 'when we have the time,' or 'when we get around to it,' could remain forever undone if that heartbeat is reached sooner than we think. The decision to excel in life, or drift aimlessly through it, rests with each of us, individually. Time is uncertain! Make your decision... **while you still can!**

The Harlem Choir Academy, and its Harlem Girls Choir, were featured on television in early 1998. Created to complement the huge success of the Harlem Boys Choir, the Girls Choir has also proven its merits. Despite their difficult lives, many coming from poverty or abusive conditions, the Girls Choir is becoming world famous. These young ladies not only sing beautifully, but sing in four other languages: German, Italian, French, and Latin! Their academic excellence is phenomenal, with 98% going on to college. When asked how she could take youth from such meager backgrounds, and help them become such achievers, the Academy director replied: "The higher you set the standard, the more they strive to reach it!"

Why not set your own high standards? Why not aim for excellence in all that you do?

God's gift to you is what you are! Your gift to God is what you become! (Author unknown)

CHAPTER THREE
IS CLOSED-MINDEDNESS CLOSING YOUR DOORS?

Bert sat in the living room of a double-wide home, on neat but inexpensive furniture, and talked to a young husband and wife while their children played nearby. They had invited him to discuss a financial diversification strategy for developing extra income. This family obviously needed to do something differently. Both parents worked, though she wanted to be a stay-home Mom. The children spent many hours with baby-sitters. Their lifestyle was lower middle-class, at best, and they appeared to just be getting by. As Bert started to explain the options, he encountered immediate resistance. Rather than attempting to first understand the choices offered them, they were throwing up barriers of absurd arguments and ridiculous excuses. Bert tried to break through their wall of thinking, then, realizing it was fruitless, politely said his good-bye. Years from now, both will probably still be working, and nothing, except age, will have changed. What's holding them back?

We all know people like this. Perhaps we're that way, ourselves. Maybe we're tempted to admire this kind of thinking as being "strong-willed," "confident," or "independent." It can even be humorous to listen to someone take a stand on an issue about which they know little. However, is it really a laughing matter, and is there harm in such an attitude? If so, who is getting hurt? In the example above, Bert might be offended, and probably felt he wasted his time by responding to their invitation. But, he wasn't the real victim... this family was the ultimate loser.

Do you know someone who avoids people, solely because of skin color, race, religion, or politics? If an acquaintance wanted to share a new and different idea with you, would you look for the first reason to reject their idea without further investigation? If you were exposed to a new business, investment, or financial concept, would you assume that it 'won't work' or 'isn't your cup of tea,' without bothering to obtain and study the facts? If the door to opportunity opened, would you automatically look for the first excuse you can find... and slam the door shut? If the answer is "yes," you could be closing your doors to growth and prosperity!

Closed-minded thinking has become epidemic in today's society! Its damage is insidious and widespread, and it threatens the very fabric upon which the United States of America was created. It is an underlying factor in every downward trend discussed in chapter one! Closed-mindedness is no laughing matter... it's a mental plague sweeping across this land and it's threatening the quality of my life, your life, and our children's lives. For this reason, we begin our study with the attitude of closed-mindedness.

Closed-mindedness... What is it, and Why do I have it?

Closed-minded thinking is narrow-minded thinking. It is an attitude and a thought process, both of which are flawed! Closed-mindedness causes us to be illogical and unwise in the way we make our decisions, thereby hampering our ability to progress. It is at the root of all racism, and has caused untold pain, anguish, and heartbreak throughout all nations and across all ages. It is a mental chain binding us to conditions of mediocrity, discontent, and poverty. Closed-mindedness partially explains why so few people truly succeed in their entire lifetimes!

A closed mind is just as the name suggests: *a mind that is **closed to**, **resistant to**, or **not receptive** to a particular subject.* We can have a closed mind to virtually any person or subject. One may be closed-minded to new ideas, as was the couple in the example above. Or, we may not be receptive to other people, usually based on some preconceived notion of what they are like. We may even close our minds against unfamiliar opportunities. Whatever the subject or issue, when we close our mind to it we are not receptive to gathering facts, evaluating evidence, or seeking the truth.

Closed-mindedness can be both a specific thought process or an attitude. All of us are capable of being selectively closed-minded on some specific subjects. An open-minded person of high integrity may be very closed-minded about a suggestion to commit a dishonest act. On the other hand, many people develop an attitude of closed-mindedness. Racism comes from such an attitude. **The person with an attitude of closed-mindedness is generally unreceptive or intolerant toward anyone and anything which is unfamiliar or which challenges their present thinking.**

A closed mind is a product of our self-esteem, education, experiences, and ignorance! We are not born closed-minded. Quite the opposite is true. Observe any infant, and you see an open mind hard at work getting into anything and everything, eager to get their hands on whatever this world offers them. Somewhere along the way into adulthood, most of us begin to shift our mental gears from an attitude of openness to one of closed-mindedness. Perhaps this is partly a defensive reaction to protect our ego. To be open-minded, we must willingly admit that we don't know everything there is to know about many subjects. The closed mind, however, assumes and acts as if it already has enough knowledge, whether it does or not. It may be ignorant... but is unwilling to admit to ignorance!

Our personal **confidence and self-esteem** may play a role in our degree of open or closed-mindedness. Our education and life experiences affect our attitude. If we are well educated and/or have generally positive experiences, we probably have a high level of confidence and self-esteem. The more comfortable we feel about ourselves, the easier it is for us to admit that we are uninformed regarding most people and subjects. Psychiatrists tell us that most people suffer from low self-esteem in our modern world. The lower our self-esteem and self-confidence, the harder it may be for us to admit that we don't know. We can begin to clothe ourselves in a facade of closed-minded thinking... assuming, deciding, and acting as if we have all the answers and don't need any more information or investigation.

Few of us are taught the hazards of being closed-minded! Virtually no school teaches anything on this subject, and few of our parents or institutions educate us because nobody taught them. We, therefore, harvest a bumper crop of this kind of thinking in today's complex society. If we don't know the dangers, and it's a natural tendency which we react to, then most of us fall further into this thought pattern. Many of us are closed-minded... because we are **unaware** of the trap and unenlightened to the consequences!

Closed-mindedness may become an **attitude habit**, and can become so ingrained in our mental processes that it becomes nearly automatic. If we have developed a habit of closed-mindedness, the subconscious nature of habits may make it difficult for us to recognize it in ourselves. Whether we recognize it or not, if a closed mind was not aware of crucial information... it remains unaware!

This brings us to the heart of closed-mindedness. A closed-minded person is consciously or subconsciously making decisions and judgments on the basis of <u>preconceived ideas, emotions</u>, and <u>previously held opinions</u>... rather than on a thorough, logical, intelligent, and sufficient investigation of the facts and truth. In those instances when the person or issue could have been important to us, a faulty decision process causes enormous harm to our future. In other words, **closed-mindedness is a thought habit whereby we base our choices and actions upon assumptions and inadequate investigation, even when the issue might be important!**

How does Closed-mindedness "Close my Doors"?

A good friend of mine, a respected orthopedic surgeon and businessman, says that **"ignorance is the foundation of all prejudice"!** <u>Ignorance</u> is defined in the dictionary as "lacking knowledge and experience," or "being unaware." <u>Prejudice</u> is defined as "having preconceived, usually unfavorable, ideas," "an opinion held in disregard of the facts which contradict it," or "intolerance or hatred." Whether the prejudice involves racism, or the subtle put-downs of someone who talks differently, or the illogical fault-finding of ideas, concepts, and opportunities that challenge our thinking... the common denominator is ignorance.

At the core of any **prejudice** are inadequate knowledge, limited experience, and lack of awareness; preconceptions, misconceptions, and opinions; and, often, intolerance or hatred. Virtually every one of these elements reflects a <u>lack of facts and truth</u>... the essence of "ignorance." Closed-minded thinking promotes ignorance! And, it is the lifeblood of prejudice because it fosters a condition of chronic ignorance toward a given issue!

With a closed mind, we **ignore or reject the information** which would have made us more knowledgeable and heightened our awareness. When we allow our mind to close to a subject, we limit our awareness of that subject to only the knowledge we already had, or to our present opinions and perceptions. The closed mind is a mind that is already made up. It does <u>not</u> want to investigate further, it does <u>not</u> want to know if it has good or bad information, it does <u>not</u> want to know if it may be wrong... it does not want to know anything more about the subject. It **assumes** it has enough information, and that it is accurate. Whatever misconceptions we may have had on that subject... continue to influence us!

Here, we need to remind ourselves that much information, many issues, and even some people are not important to us! Regardless of who we are or what we do, there will always be matters which are trivial, unnecessary, and insignificant to us, individually. Such matters amount to a waste of our time if we get caught up in them. One such example would be 'junk mail.' Most adults get literally dozens of junk mail items throughout the year. The major portion of such mail is totally worthless to us, yet, we waste some amount of our time opening it just to be sure. Every one of us will always be ignorant of most people and subjects. In many instances, that's just as well! They simply don't affect us.

However, if we are to grasp the full significance of "closed-mindedness," we must understand that **there are subjects which <u>are</u> important to us... whether we recognize them or not!** Closed-mindedness hurts us because it causes us to not recognize nor investigate many subjects which could have been beneficial for ourselves and our loved ones. Therefore, opportunities... for love, friendship, happiness, prosperity... are lost without us even knowing they got away!

The point of this whole discussion is... **how do you know?** How do we make a distinction between the mass of trivia, and the things that might matter to us? Perhaps we could put all issues into three categories. One category would be those things that we know instantly are of no value or consequence to us... the things we can ignore or reject with complete confidence. An example is an offer to commit a crime; we know we can be totally closed to it. A second category consists of those things that we automatically know could matter, and that we undoubtedly need to be open-minded to. For example, we know without question that we should fully investigate if our doctor says we may have a major illness. The third category, though, is the "uncertain area," where the issues may or may not be important. Examples in this category are new concepts, investments, people, ideas, businesses, and opportunities. This is by far the largest category.

The "uncertain area" is where most of us are "blowing it"! Here is where most of life's opportunities are. Here are most of the people and their ideas that could improve the quality of our lives. Here are our greatest chances for achieving enduring peace, contentment, happiness, and prosperity. But, those things that we cannot be immediately sure about are the very things that a closed mind turns its back on. Many of these 'things' that we ignore and reject could do wonders for our lives, if we only checked them out with an open mind! And, taking the time and making the effort to investigate is the only way we'll know.

If the subject is potentially important, the only thing

worse than being uninformed, is allowing ourselves to remain uninformed!

Human Achievement and Happiness are the Result of Three Ingredients!

One: Ideas start first in somebody's mind and form the substance of every human creation and accomplishment! A simple tool, such as a pencil, and a complex machine like the space shuttle, share the common element of thought. Ideas, thoughts, and concepts become the seeds which ultimately produce the realities of the human experience. We must control our random thought processes, while putting good thoughts... ideas, concepts, information... into our minds. The good ideas of others may become our good ideas, and may bear good fruit for us.

Two: Opportunity is defined by Webster's as "a combination of circumstances favorable for the purpose," or a "good chance." While small opportunities flit through our lives constantly, focus on the potentially life-changing opportunities, when circumstances create a chance to truly improve our lives. These are not nearly in such abundance. Most people likely have only a few dozen major opportunities in their entire lifetimes. Whether these are opportunities to establish relationships with key people, a big career or job decision, a shot at furthering your education, a business, or a chance to relocate, they are few and often far between. Many are even disguised and may go unrecognized. Most of us cannot afford to let even one life-changing possibility get away from us.

Three: People play a part, no matter what we do or plan to do. We may need a partner, investors, or managers and employees, in order to start a new business. The business itself will need suppliers and customers. We may have an employer and supervisors, if we work for another. Our idea may require scientists, engineers, researchers, teachers, administrators, and others, if it is to become reality. Every human accomplishment

27

requires the willing cooperation, alliance, or mentorship of another person! For you and I to succeed in life, we must rely on the knowledge, friendship, cooperation, skills, and creations of other people.

Closed-minded thinking is so harmful to us because it causes us to ignore or dismiss, without investigation, these three basic elements we must have in order to maximize our lives! We cut ourselves with our own sword, because we deny ourselves the benefits we might have gained from exposure to new ideas, opportunities, and people! We do it to ourselves, because we allow ourselves to remain uneducated, uninformed, unaware... when we should be learning!

Why be Open-minded?

We cannot remove our barriers of ignorance about a given person or subject unless we are open and willing to do so. We must **decide** to adequately investigate and understand an individual or issue. Therefore, "open-mindedness" could be described as "**choosing** to become informed and aware regarding potentially significant or important matters," or "**choosing** to adequately research and analyze the facts and truth before making critical judgments."

Obviously, we don't have enough time in our lives to investigate every idea, opportunity, or person in the world. Therefore, we need to have a vision and goals for our own life which can help us recognize those elements which might be of value to us, individually. If we even suspect that a person or subject may contribute in a significant way to our goals, dreams, knowledge, friendship, prosperity, or happiness, we should strongly consider putting aside whatever prejudices and preconceptions we may have and investigate adequately. Isn't that what we call **'wisdom'**? **How else will we know?**

An open mind is a prerequisite to acquiring the knowledge and making the personal preparations to achieve any of life's finer qualities. Whether we want to create greater harmony in

28

our relationships, develop better health, become more charitable, become financially wealthy, or develop spiritually... our beginning must involve an attitude and spirit of 'open-mindedness'. Only the person with an open mind will first recognize, then take full advantage of, life's opportunities.

In his 1965 book, *The Master Key to Riches*, Napoleon Hill lists "an open mind on all subjects" as one of the twelve riches of life. He says that:

Tolerance, which is among the higher attributes of culture, is expressed only by the person who holds an open mind on all subjects at all times. And it is only the man with an open mind who becomes truly educated and who is thus prepared to avail himself of the greater riches of life....

The greatest irony of closed-minded thinking is that we hurt ourselves (and our loved ones) as much or more than we hurt the other guy. Such an attitude limits our ability to learn, grow and achieve toward our fullest potential.

The only route to lasting peace, true happiness, and long-term success... is the pathway through an open mind!

CHAPTER FOUR
FEARFUL THAT YOU'RE AFRAID?

I stared for the umpteenth time at the sign above the mailboxes in our college dormitory at the University of Nebraska. It said: *"Baseball tryouts today at 3:00 PM."* I wanted nothing more than to play baseball, and to play for my beloved Cornhuskers would be a dream come true. However, I came from such a small cattle ranching town and community in Western Nebraska that our little league team didn't have enough boys... many Dads had to fill in. My Dad would play catch with me by the hour, whenever we could find the time outside of ranch work. My arm was very strong and accurate, and I became the pitcher. The fathers soon had to always take the position of "catcher," because I threw too hard for the kids to handle. Our wonderful neighbor, Bob Merrihew, usually acted as catcher, and had to fit a foam pad into his catcher's mitt, to help cushion my throws. Despite the extra pad, his hand would still swell up as if stung by a wasp. Few adults, and almost none of the kids, could hit against me, effectively. You can see my dilemma... natural ability, but limited opportunity to develop it. I looked at the sign for the last time, gathered up my books, and walked sadly to class... resigned to not tryout for the team.

Many years later, I sat in a large audience anxiously waiting for the next speaker. He was a former rodeo bull rider and a reigning state body-building champion. He was going to talk about how he had progressed on the road toward the American dream. This man was one of those we'd often say "had it all." As he began to speak, something unexpected happened: his voice quivered and faltered so badly, that he could literally not find the words. Before thousands of people, he stood on the stage... and struggled mightily to say anything!

The examples above have one element in common: **fear!** I wish I could ask for your sympathy, in my personal example, because of God's cruel trick of having my birth in a small town... but that would be living a lie. The simple truth is that I allowed fear to stop me from trying out. Fear also gripped the tongue of the bull-rider, and a man who could tie himself atop a 2000 pound animal could not control the fear of standing and speaking before a group of people. The message is this: *fear is a common factor we all face, and it will prevent us from doing the things we want to do, if we allow it to!*

What's this "Fear" that I'm Afraid of?

Fear is a powerful enemy of success partly because it is like a chameleon, it can change complexion and is often hard to recognize. It attacks us from many different directions, and we often don't even know it's got us. A portion of its power comes from the fact that even when we do recognize it, because of our "manliness" or ego, we refuse to acknowledge it and we hide it behind other names or excuses. Thus, we allow it to run freely and do its dirty work untethered. Let's look at some of the facets of this monster which holds us back.

There are basic fears which affect all of us, to varying degrees: the fears of death, injury, ill health, old age, loss of love, loss of freedom, and criticism. Some of these fears are healthy, if kept in balance, and prevent us from taking unworthy and unnecessary risks which could result in loss, pain, injury or death. When unbalanced, though, these fears can cause extreme behavior. In his old age, billionaire Howard Hughes became so obsessed with health that he became a total recluse. Other, more specific, fears may hinder us greatly at a particular time or occasion, or not at all. These are the fears of speaking in public, flying, being in close places, water, fire, falling, and many other phobias too numerous to name. The fears that we need to concentrate on are more insidious, yet very common challenges to individual growth and achievement.

The four fears we'll focus on are what we may call **lifestyle fears**. Many of us will experience these to varying degrees, especially when considering changes and options that affect our personal achievements or finances. These fears seldom involve choices that might harm us physically, so are not normally a direct threat to our health. Lifestyle fears usually pertain to decisions about money matters, job or occupation issues, and choices regarding our self-development and individual success. Such fears are more subtle and harder to recognize and control because they involve threats to our <u>ego and psyche</u>, rather than to our bodies. *They do their dirty work when **they paralyze us into inaction**, and **cause us to quit before we even start**. Often, because of these four robbers, we don't even try! That's their danger!*

Failure!

We'll first discuss the fear which kept me from possibly playing baseball. This thief might have cost me the chance to play college ball, and millions of dollars in potential earnings as a professional. My entire adult life could be drastically different. I'll never know... because I didn't try! That's what the **fear of failure** does to us! This one fear is probably singularly responsible for more unused, unreached, and dismissed potential... than any other fear. In the areas of personal growth, achievement, relationships, work, and finances, few factors have a greater negative impact!

Do not let this point slip by you! Understand that it is not actual failure that is stopping us... it is the **fear** of failure! **FEARING that we might not succeed, we talk ourselves out of trying.** That is the tragedy of this fear, and the other three we'll discuss.

Failure is a dirty word in our culture. In our schools, a failing grade on a test, paper or in a course is cause for shame, anger, a lecture, scolding, loss of privileges, staying late, and so forth. When we talk of a failed relationship, we are talking of one which ended, often with bad feelings. Mechanical failures cause automobile recalls which cost millions, and bring down airplanes with great loss of life. Failure is seen by most Americans as a permanent condition which taints us, perhaps even for life! But, should it?

32

History offers much evidence to the contrary. Professional sports teams and individuals lose games during the season, yet fight on to become World Champions. The University of Nebraska football team had developed a ten year stigma for not winning the big game. Then, in 1995, 1996, and 1998, they won national championships, a feat equaled by only a handful of other teams. Michael Jordan, arguably the greatest of all basketball players, doesn't shoot and rebound at 100%. Even he misses! Thomas Edison, the inventor of the electric light bulb, failed in thousands of attempts, before he finally found the right combination... and succeeded.

One of our greatest Presidents, Abraham Lincoln, was a dismal failure at business and several attempts at political offices, as well as suffering personal setbacks of death and mental illness within his immediate family, before he was elected to the Presidency. During the carving of Mount Rushmore, Borghlum had to literally change faces from one mountain to another, years into the project, because he determined the first arrangement would not work. We could go on and on, with countless examples, but the point is hopefully clear that *failures are only temporary stepping stones which we can learn from, and use to propel us more wisely toward success. An unsuccessful attempt is not total* **failure***, until _we_ decide it is permanent!*

When someone tries and fails, rather than condemn them, we should congratulate them for having the guts and gumption to try! We should point out that they are now wiser and one step closer to success. Thank the Lord that one more person had the courage, ambition, confidence, and determination to attempt to do something worth doing. We should celebrate when a person picks himself or herself up, dusts off their boots, and tries again! When that happens, failure was not permanent and did not win... the person is a winner!

You and I must not allow ourselves, our children, nor our friends to fear failure to the extent that it stops us from trying! When that happens, it is one of life's tragedies, because one more achievement, however big or small, may be lost. *Let's help each other see failure for what it is, just a learning experience and a chance to do it again smarter. Failing and quitting may be despised at times, but it's far worse to not try at all!*

Criticism!

Another fear which is a significant deterrent to human growth and improvement... financial, spiritual, health, or otherwise... is the **fear of criticism!** This has been a big handicap in my life, because I spent many of my years overly concerned about what others thought of me. Now, let's be honest: nobody likes to be criticized. We would probably be certifiably 'nuts' if we did like it. It can be frustrating, irritating, and can at times hurt. However, we need to unemotionally consider just how important criticism is. The answer is: not very!

In the first place, if we allow a fear of criticism to stop us from trying, we are <u>assuming</u> that someone will actually criticize us, and that it matters. Most of the people who might scrutinize us, probably won't say anything at all. So, why get worked up and lose sleep over what somebody 'might' say? You'd probably be surprised, and maybe even offended, to know how few people care what you do! Most of us have too many problems and concerns of our own, to worry about what the other guy is doing, even if we care about them. It is unwise to <u>assume</u> that someone will disapprove of us, and let that fear stop us from trying.

Secondly, we need to evaluate whether criticism matters. Here, we make a distinction between requested opinions or feedback, and <u>unsolicited</u> criticism. When we ask a person, whose opinion we value, for judgment or critique, we are seeking inputs and advice with which we expect to benefit. Unsolicited criticism, however, is frequently founded in a negative attitude or personal agenda. I have found that the more open, educated, and wise a person is, and the more successful they are in life, the less apt they are to criticize anyone at all! We usually ask these people for opinions and feedback, because their evaluations are meaningful. I've also observed that the opposite is true: *the less educated, less open-minded, less successful, and the more ignorant someone is...* ***the more they justify their own mediocrity by finding fault with others!*** Therefore, the large majority of criticism we receive will come from the second group, and is of little or no value. Why let <u>them</u> deter us? A good rule of thumb is: check the source.

Rejection!

The next lifestyle fear is the **fear of rejection.** Like criticism, it is not fun to be rejected by someone whose acceptance we wanted or needed. Sales people look this fear in the eyes every time they approach a contact. The important thing is to keep a balanced perspective. It is a fact that not everyone is going to be interested in any one thing all the time. For some, the issue, item, person, circumstances, or timing will simply be wrong. Jesus, Himself, was criticized and rejected by many whom he sought to lead to God. Why would you and I expect to have a better record than Jesus?

We will have successes with those for whom the issue, item, people, circumstances, and timing are right! If our product, services, ideas, and motives are worthwhile, (and, unfortunately, even if they're worthless) consistent persistence will lead us to those who do not reject us. Every marriage is proof of the power of persistence! For more proof, look at Jim Jones, who led hundreds to their suicides in Guyana. Better yet, consider that a man in California convinced 38 people to take their lives in the belief that a comet would pick them up. If these people can find others who passionately accept their position or idea, you and I can find those who will support our ideas!

Fearing rejection, and not acting as a result of that fear, is the loser's way out! People will say "no" to our ideas and offerings from time to time. There is absolutely nothing you nor I can do to make it otherwise. To expect perfection is to deny reality, a definition of insanity. It makes no sense to base our decisions on illogical and unrealistic expectations, especially concerning matters of personal enrichment. The only way to get around the fear of rejection, is to get prepared and get going, then continue learning and going! *Get a winner's attitude!*

Change!

Some of us **fear change!** We don't want our boat rocked, we just want life to stay the way we perceived it to be. Sometimes, life isn't even all that great, but it is good enough that we don't want any interruptions to our routine. If you relate to this, you need to do some serious thinking.

Change is a fact of life! This earth, and everything on it, are in a constant state of change and evolution. It does not matter if the change is for better, or for worse, it is occurring regardless. Our forests are declining and our deserts growing, with every passing day. Biologists tell us that hundreds, if not thousands, of species become extinct, daily. The atmosphere does not have the same oxygen content, or chemical composition, that it had during the dinosaur era. Our fruits and vegetables are not as nutritious as they were a hundred years ago, because of soil depletion. Mankind is building and expanding roads, bridges, monuments, cities, and transportation capacity at a hectic pace.

Each year, individuals push the limits of human capability to previously unbelievable levels. Every day, new ideas, concepts and opportunities become available. Products and services improve constantly. Communications are tremendous today, compared to even a decade ago. And, one of the greatest of all changes is happening to us right now. From the day we were born, our body and mind have been in a slow but steady process of change. It began with the miracle of conception and birth, and will end with our death. This life-altering process takes place within us, totally beyond our control!

Since change is going to happen, whether we participate willingly or not, we may as well participate by choice! Observe any highly successful person, and you'll find that they accept, embrace, anticipate, and use change to their advantage, thereby making the most of life's twists and turns. *There is probably nothing more illogical, than to allow a fear of or resistance to **change** to control our decisions!*

OK, I'm Afraid! What do I do?

In our search for more meaning, satisfaction, and quality in our lives, we are going to run headlong into fears. When we do, they will stop us in our tracks, and trap us where we are, unless we overcome them. In the beginning of this chapter, I gave an example of a bull rider who had extreme fear of public speaking. The rest of the story is that he overcame his fear! Rather than let it beat him, as many would have done by leaving the stage in shame and never trying again, this man reached for the words until they came. By doing what he feared, he put his fear in its proper place, and is now a leader and a fine speaker. And, there you have the key...**the only way to combat fear is to take the action in spite of it!**

The fears we are discussing are probably about 90% perception, 10% reality! The vaccination isn't half as bad, once over, that it seemed before the needle went in. The same is true for many other fears. Usually, if what we fear happens at all, it is not nearly as severe and painful as we <u>imagined</u> it would be. Fear is a healthy emotion, when it causes us to investigate, evaluate, study and prepare for a worthwhile risk, adequately, before taking it on. Because we respond to healthy fear with more thought and preparation for the risks we expect, our chances of succeeding are significantly better than if we just jumped in with no preparation. Even if the worst happens, we probably still make progress!

Fear becomes unhealthy when it stops us from taking <u>worthwhile</u> and <u>acceptable</u> risks! Since most lifestyle fears are about 90% perception, the longer we wait, wonder, ponder, and worry, the more our imagination builds up what we fear. Today's mole hill becomes a mountain after a month of worrying about it! There is a point at which we are as prepared as we need to be, for the risk we face. Beyond that point, further delay only heightens our imagination, strengthens our fear, and reduces our resolve to overcome it. We come again to the key: **we must take action if we are to defeat fear!** By taking the step we fear, just as soon as we are reasonably prepared, we automatically reduce that fear to the 10% reality level, the acceptable risk, which our logic has determined is worth the effort.

Keep in mind that life itself is a 100% risk. None of us will get out of it alive! So, how bad can all the other stuff be? Every single thing we will consider doing will have some risk. The greater the potential reward, the greater the associated risk. Going for that golden opportunity will also bring the risk of possibly failing, being criticized and put down, being outright rejected by some who refuse to understand, and will always involve change. However, are we going to run from every opportunity just because of those fears? Or, are we going to see them for what they are... success robbers and mediocrity keepers... and tackle them head-on?

David J. Swartz says, in his 1959 book, *The Magic of Thinking Big*: **"Action cures fear"**!

"He has not learned the first lesson of life who does not every day surmount a fear." (Ralph Waldo Emerson)

"If you want to be rewarded, you have to be willing to fail." (Scott Hamilton, figure skating champion, discussing the 1998 Winter Olympians)

"Never let the fear of striking out get in your way." (George Herman "Babe" Ruth)

CHAPTER FIVE
LOSING TO YOUR OWN GAME.... EXCUSE-ITIS?

The 70-year-old gentleman was still getting around fairly well. Though he had been retired for several years, his marriage recently failed, and he was now facing life alone and in financial trouble. A friend offered to help him start a business, and was willing to work with him and teach him. This business was well within the senior citizen's experience, financial and physical capabilities. Since it involved working with people, it would have been very positive for the older fellow, who desperately needed to regain his confidence and social skills. After an initial interest and a feeble attempt to get started, though, the gentleman told his friend: "I'm just too old to do this. I have no choice but to give up!" And, he gave up... on both business and life!

I had a notion for nearly two years to write a book, but kept putting it off because I thought I was "too busy." I was working two businesses, doing considerable remodeling and restoration on our old house, and doing some speaking. As I pondered whether to try my hand at motivational writing, I kept telling myself: "I just don't have the time right now." The reality, though, was that I could have done it if I had just used my time more effectively!

A humorous story goes like this: "This guy went next door to borrow his neighbor's chainsaw. Upon hearing the request, the neighbor said he really couldn't loan the chainsaw, because he needed to make some vegetable stew tomorrow. The borrower-to-be then asked 'what does your making stew have to do with loaning me your saw?' His neighbor replied: 'it doesn't have anything to do with it, but if I don't want to loan you my saw, one excuse is as good as another!'"

The message I hope to convey in these examples is that, when it comes to making excuses, one excuse is just as good (and lame) as another! Sadly, the reality in modern day America is that we have acquired the chronic habit of making excuses.

The malady of **excuse-itis** has become another thief which, for most of us, is robbing us and holding us back.

Excuse-itis... Just what is it?

Let's first establish a reference for this chapter. Excuse is defined in the dictionary as: "to justify (one's position or actions)," or "something which releases us from an obligation," or "a pretext ('a false reason put forth to hide the real one')." As we will discuss 'excuses', all three definitions may apply at times, but generally we're talking about "false reasons put forth to hide the real ones." *"Excuse-itis" is a chronic habit of making excuses.*

Since we are exploring those mental roadblocks which prevent us from doing more with our lives, then the excuses we want to focus on are those which hold us back. These are excuses which get us out of doing something that we probably should be doing. Also, excuses can be used to justify doing something that we probably should not do. So, for the purposes of this chapter, *"'Excuse-itis' is a chronic habit of making excuses to avoid things that we could and probably should do, or to justify doing things that we probably shouldn't do!"*

We've all heard, and probably made, many excuses. The usual excuse has the message: "too much of something, prevents me from doing this." For the older man above, he was "too old to try to change his life for the better." In my case, I thought I was "too busy to write." In the humorous quip, the neighbor was "too involved in making stew, to loan his saw." As you perhaps consider your own excuses, let's analyze some of the elements which characterize an excuse. In the excuse examples used above, note that the action called for was within the ability of each person. The old friend had the means, ability, help, and need to pursue his business; I had the desire and ability to attempt to write a book; and the neighbor could have loaned his chainsaw. If we were truly unable to take the called-for action, we'd have no need to make an excuse. We could just tell the truth: "I can't do it." One common element, then, is: *an excuse **always** involves something we **could** do, if we chose to!*

A second trait of excuse-itis is that we probably should take the action being excused! If someone tells me I should mug an elderly lady, and I tell them "I'm too busy," that's a valid, though incomplete, reason because it was an act that I should not do. While this is an excuse, it's a good one that reflects integrity. I should not consider the alternative of mugging the lady. However, if my wife tells me I should have a talk with my daughter, whom I haven't seen in a long time, and I tell her I'm just "too tired" ... that's almost always a lame excuse! The fact is, if it's important enough, I can find the energy. I probably should call my daughter. As the husband, father, and leader of my family, I owe it to them to constantly strive for quality in their lives. Therefore, the actions being excused by the habit of excuse-itis are, to some degree... **obligations!**

The third element of an excuse is the reason, or **pretext**, given to justify releasing us from the obligation. The pretext can be many things. As offered above, it could be "too old," "too busy," "too fat," "too thin," "too young," "not enough money," "not the right amount of education," "overly qualified," "poor health," "handicapped," etc. etc. *When we make an "excuse," it matters little what our justification is;* **It's usually not true!**

The fact is, there are very few things that we can't do if we really want to! For proof, study the people who accomplish worthwhile things. In virtually every occupation and endeavor, you can find those who are "too old" or "too young," "too fat" or "too thin," "uneducated" or "overly qualified," in "poor health," "physically handicapped" and on and on... yet, they're doing worthwhile and often spectacular achievements! For literally every excuse one man makes, another with worse challenges is doing what the first one said he could not do. In the Air Force, we said "If you want to get something done, give it to a busy person... they don't have time to make excuses, they just do it!" *The reasons given for our excuses rarely stand up to close scrutiny. That's why we call them...* **excuses!**

We can put these three characteristics together, and we have the foundation of excuse-itis, which keeps us from doing more with our lives. When you and I <u>could do something</u>, which we are at least somewhat <u>obligated to do or attempt to do</u>, and we <u>justify not doing it</u> by reasoning that is, at best, only partially true, or more likely untrue... **we are making excuses.**

Excuse-itis is the chronic habit of making excuses to justify being less responsible, less accountable, and less productive with our lives!

The "Excuse of the '90's"

As a representative example, let's concentrate on a common excuse, the **excuse of the 90's**, which demonstrates the underlying dishonesty in all excuses. This is: "I'm too busy!", or variations of "I don't have the time!". In the hectic arena of modern life, this one excuse is the most overworked of all. It's overworked, because it's seems acceptable and believable. But, is it?

Lack of time seems like a good excuse because most people <u>are</u> busy! In the typical 1990's American family, both husband and wife work full-time jobs, sometimes six days a week. If either are in a corporate leadership role, the demands of employment are even more intense. Add children, and you have a family that's going in many different directions at a high rate of speed. Those who relate to this can validate that they are very <u>busy</u>!

Let's look a little deeper, though! One question begs for an honest answer. Are we busy doing the most important and meaningful activities, or are we busy doing a lot of 'stuff' which isn't necessary or critical? In the workplace, much time and effort is frequently wasted on "make work," unimportant projects, long coffee breaks and lunches, and mismanagement. In some positions, we expect to go early and stay late as a matter of perceived policy, whether we need to, or not. Employers, studies, and time management experts all suggest that most of us could perform more efficiently and effectively, by improving time management and discipline! *Are we productively busy? Or, do we just think we're busy... because we don't use our time wisely?*

Are we leading and managing our families efficiently? A considerable body of evidence suggests not! Evidence indicates that our children will develop into healthier and more well-rounded young adults, if they have quality time with their parents. Perhaps, we do them an injustice by allowing them to be involved in too many activities? Are we really using activities as "child care"? If we weren't shuffling our children to so many places, could we manage our time better, while giving them more quality time with us?

How do you spend your discretionary time? Many people are well-intentioned social butterflies, flitting between parties, meetings, and recreational activities. Some are sports enthusiasts. Others become enamored with volunteer-ism. In addition, surveys show that the average American spends as much time watching television as they do at work. Do these activities actually benefit us, or our families, or take us closer to our goals? We do need relaxation time, outside interests, hobbies, and volunteers. However, some aspects of our life are too important to ignore, or to allow lesser distractions to take priority! *If we prioritized our goals and our time, most of us would realize we're spending too much time on activities having little value for our future!*

Human nature being what it is, you and I will do what we want to do! If you're a college football fan, as we are, you'll find a way to watch the "big game." My Dad was an avid fan, and a cattle rancher. As a rancher, you work when you need to, frequently seven days a week. Dad, however, would start work at 4:00 AM, or work till 10:00 PM, before, after, and the day

43

of, if that's what was required to watch "the game." My parents were major supporters when we played high school sports. They'd do whatever it took so they could be at our games. In rural West Nebraska, this often involved many hour drives, to and from distant towns. Their example is true for all of us. When we desire to make the time, we make it. If we're honest, we can probably find the time to do that thing we just said we were too busy to do... if we want to!

Lastly, you and I, and every drunk, bum, philanthropist, and person of mediocrity or wealth, share one thing in common. *Regardless of our status in life, **we each have 24 hours in every day!*** No more, no less. The busy person has exactly the same amount of daily time as does the not-so-busy one. The person of wealth and power has no more time in their day, than does the person of poverty and obscurity. In addition, not one of us knows how many days we have left.

The fact is this: you have just as many hours in your day as does everyone else, and you're probably no busier than most other people think they are. Can you really justify that next excuse of "I don't have the time"? The only things that differentiate **success** from **failure**, where our time is concerned, are **setting priorities** and **managing our time accordingly!** If we aren't doing both, we have little validity in using time as an excuse.

Why Should I Defeat "Excuse-itis"?

Perhaps by now, you sense that excuse-itis is harmful? First, we lower our self-esteem, and our reputation, by *doing less than we are capable of doing.* Secondly, *an excuse is essentially a lie*, and we not only develop and justify a *habit of dishonesty*, but we *lessen our character* because we know we're lying. In the final analysis, *we fail to meet the expectations* of friends, family, associates, customers, employees, our employer, even of ourselves and our loved ones, by virtue of our excuses. Regardless of the issue or reason, when we make excuses, especially to self and family, *we limit our potential* for achievement, improvement, and happiness!

Excuses, commonplace as they have become, seldom fool anyone! Do we husbands honestly believe we're fooling our wives, when we back out of the obligations we make to them because "we're too busy"? Even if we are busy, do you think they appreciate our priorities? The truth is that we probably don't convince the other person with our excuses. Prevalent as it is, excuse-itis is easy to identify in the other fellow. The only person we may truly fool... is **ourselves**, by thinking the other guy bought our excuse!

There is a principle of success (and failure) called "autosuggestion" or "self-talk." We all mentally talk to ourselves all the time. Autosuggestion occurs when we continually repeat a thought or type of thoughts. Communism survived many years, because the doctrine was repeated until the Soviet people accepted it without question. Often, convicted criminals deny their crime to the grave, because they repeatedly justified their actions, until they believed themselves. Autosuggestion is literally "self brainwashing," and can be used positively, with motivational and worthy thoughts, or negatively, with destructive thoughts. By autosuggestion, any lie can be accepted by the person who repeats it frequently and with conviction.

We have already shown that excuse-itis is inherently dishonest. If you continually make the same excuse (for instance: "I'm too old!"), autosuggestion will eventually convince you that your pretext is valid, even if you knew at first it was not. You will start to believe your own lie... and actually conclude that "I <u>am</u> too old!". This explains why David J. Schwartz, in his 1959 book, *The Magic Of Thinking Big,* refers to our excuse habit as "the failure disease." Once a man acquires the "failure disease," he believes his own excuses, thereby justifying doing less with his life than what he is capable of doing. He also condemns those who depend on him, his wife and children, to the same fate... mediocrity!

See "excuse-itis" for what it is... an attitude of dishonesty and failure! When we have an opportunity to make a difference, you and I owe it to ourselves, our loved ones, and to other people, to honestly evaluate whether we can, and should. And, if we can, and should... then do. Nobody deserves an excuse. And, **You don't deserve to be a failure!**

CHAPTER SIX
"ACCOUNTABLE"... TO NOBODY?

I sat in the coffee shop, alone, for 30 minutes, waiting for a recent acquaintance to show up. I had met him a few weeks before, and wanted to get to know him better. We had arranged to meet for coffee. Now, after working my schedule accordingly and making the trip across town, he was nowhere to be seen. I gave up and went home, having wasted nearly two hours of my time! He never called to apologize or explain his absence.

In another instance, the wife was anxious to go out for dinner, as her husband had told her days earlier they would. Finding himself running behind at work, though, on the afternoon they were to go out, he told her they couldn't. While she didn't say anything, for the next couple of days she was distant and moody. Something was obviously bothering her.

A business agreed to sell a sizable order of materials to a distant business associate. The customer was expected to send their payment immediately, since all transactions were in cash. Six weeks later, they still had not sent their payment, and not only was the situation starting to strain the relationship, but it had left the business in a very tenuous financial condition.

During recent years, high-profile criminal murder trials captured the headlines and the attention across this country. In several, feelings were strong with regard to believed guilt or innocence. At least two caused a national, and in one case an international, furor when the accused were acquitted, or sentences were drastically reduced from what many believed appropriate. The reason behind such feelings comes down to an issue of accountability. For many, our confidence in the United States criminal justice system was severely damaged by a perception that people were not being held accountable, even for murder.

You and I could probably spend days sharing such incidents. Lack of **accountability** is a serious problem in today's society, and has a cancerous effect upon our ability to lead full and productive lives! In this chapter, we'll try to understand the attitude of **unaccountability.**

What are we talking about?

First, we'll focus on accountability. Webster's Dictionary says that to be accountable is to be "responsible, liable, and explainable." If one is accountable, they say what they mean, do what they say they're going to do, do what they ought to do, and accept responsibility for their actions. Accountability is not something we're born with, it is a learned behavior and attitude which ultimately reflects our integrity and character. *In short, 'accountability' is simply a matter of doing the right thing, and being a person of our word!*

In contrast, unaccountability is not being responsible, liable, or explainable. Like most personal attitudes and qualities, there are varying levels of unaccountability. Standing someone up for coffee isn't nearly as serious as failing to keep our word to our spouse. Neither are as outrageous as ignoring a debt, or committing a crime. In all cases, though, an *'unaccountable' person does not take responsibility for their words or actions.*

Isn't anyone responsible anymore?

In rural west Nebraska, it was said that a man's word and handshake were his bond. Dad always said if he couldn't take a man at his word, he couldn't trust his signature either. Over the years, however, our sense of integrity, even at the lowest levels of accountability, seems to have drastically declined! Today, people matter-of-factly ignore appointments they've made, forget about commitments, and deny their responsibility in all kinds of situations. There are too many examples of individuals committing, and getting away with, horrendous crimes. Sometimes, it seems that our judicial process first looks for reasons to excuse the accused's behavior, rather than hold them accountable for it.

Acquittals have resulted from defenses which passed the blame to parents, music, society, even to diet. All across this land, individuals and families live and act is if they have the right to be cared for by society. For some, their major goal seems to be qualifying for social 'entitlements' programs. Everywhere we look, someone is saying "it wasn't my fault." Even our highest government leaders routinely justify their actions, which often cost us millions, by pointing their finger at someone else. As we listen to instance after instance of guilt-laying and blaming, one can start to believe: The devil made me do it! (Since nobody else seems to be responsible).

When words are only words!

There is no doubt about the unaccountability of murder! People die because another person is not responsible to the standards of society and human decency. Consider, though, the effects we have on others *just by not being true to our words!* A simple thing like being stood up when meeting someone for coffee, still leaves a negative impression. In the first anecdote, I would have adjusted my work and priorities, cleaned up, dressed appropriately, and traveled to and from the coffee house. With the waiting, uncertainty, money spent unnecessarily, and the lack of an apology or explanation... you have an irritating situation. I would be less likely to believe him in the future, regardless of what he told me. He damaged his credibility with me. If he had a practice or business, he probably lost my future patronage. Since he didn't respect my time, which is valuable to me, nor explain his absence and apologize, insult is added to irritation. All this, just because he wasn't a man of his word!

Many times, we tell our spouses and children we'll do something with them, and think nothing of changing plans because 'something came up.' Our spouses and children expect a different level of integrity from us, where they're concerned. Failing to keep our word to them, regardless of the issue, does matter, whether they tell us or not. Their position demands a priority above nearly everything else! If we let them down, we give the impression that they aren't significant. Not only does this hurt their feelings, but it weakens their sense of security, importance, faith, and love. If we allow such qualities to falter in our relationships, the relationships themselves will undoubtedly falter as well! *If our families can't trust our word, what can they trust about us?*

Failing to keep our word and to take responsibility for our actions needs to be seen clearly for what it is: **lack of integrity!** It calls into question our honesty, believability, trustworthiness, and accountability. When we don't keep our word to family, friends, and loved ones, it causes them to question our sincerity and doubt if they matter to us. Whenever we allow such thoughts to enter the minds of those we have dealings or relationships with, we put them on the defensive and place ourselves at a disadvantage. We lower their respect for us thereby jeopardizing the professional or personal relationships we might have had with them. The more frequent our infractions, the greater the damage we do... when our words are only words!

The Blame Game!

Some of us have the habit of never accepting responsibility for our circumstances and always blaming someone else. One only has to observe our elected government officials to study the blame game in action. Rare is the congressman or senator who will admit to wrongdoing or poor judgment. Billions of dollars are wasted trying to fix fault and blame on someone else, with special prosecutors becoming as common on Capitol Hill as the Congress itself. We can also observe the blame game in our judicial system. There, one can observe people who, despite overwhelming evidence, continue to deny they did anything wrong. And, before we become preoccupied with pointing our fingers at everyone else, you and I play the blame game far too often as well! Spend time in any coffee shop, lounge, or bar, and you'll hear us complaining about what somebody, or the government, is doing to us (of course, we're not responsible).

The World owes Me a Living!

Probably every large family has at least one member who has turned over their responsibilities to someone else. This person is frequently found unemployed (for reasons beyond his control, of course), on public assistance of some kind, or living with other family members. This man or woman always has a reason why they can't do more for themselves, and it often involves the government, the 'system,' employers, or something else which is 'keeping them down.' Rarely, if ever, does our friend even consider that their own bad decisions and refusal to take responsibility for their life are part of the problem.

The person who believes he's owed a living is a person who can rationalize using and cheating others. Believing that someone else's assets should be ours, we can justify not repaying debts, not paying for purchases, dragging out our obligations indefinitely, and even outright theft. This kind of man asks for help, but seems unwilling to give help in return. He is a <u>taker</u>, rarely a <u>giver</u>.

Before you and I get too smug about those who fit this description, we also need to look in the mirror! Otherwise good men and women complain about all kinds of things and people who are not doing enough for us. 'They' should lower our taxes, pay us more, pay our college expenses, provide better insurance for us, and so forth. These are challenges that nearly all of us face occasionally. The question we need to ask ourselves is: *what are <u>we</u> doing about it?* Are we educating ourselves so we'll be more competitive for better paying positions? Have we looked into ways to reduce our tax liability, or to leverage our income more effectively? Do we educate ourselves on the issues, and vote? *If you and I have challenges that we're only belly-aching about, and not doing anything to try to solve, we're no better than the guy who's on his 200th month of welfare. He probably thinks the world* *should fix his problems, too!*

Why be accountable? Nobody else is!

Lack of accountability has become so commonplace in our society, that many of us don't even get upset when the other fellow let's us down. In a perverse way, we almost expect it; therefore, we just tend to accept it as being the way it is. It's too easy to rationalize the attitude that, since nobody else keeps their word, I'm not going to keep my word, either! Before you adopt that attitude, though, why not look for the opportunity to benefit from a higher standard?

When we're not accountable to other people, we do more than irritate them and cause them to mistrust us! Since the attitude of unaccountability results in dishonesty, broken promises, lack of integrity, lies, failure to keep our commitments, and failure to take responsibility for our actions... it will weaken our character and sense of self-worth. A persistent habit of not being accountable will soon become the norm for our subconscious mind. When we are no longer concerned about being reliable to others, neither will we be responsible to ourselves. Once we become conditioned to accept this character flaw, we have adopted another failure disease, and it will limit our potential for success and happiness!

The greatest reason to be accountable in all ways at all times, despite what the rest of society is doing, is to vastly expand our potential for succeeding! Lack of accountability is nothing more than a lax attitude toward our responsibilities to other people, and to ourselves. Similarly, accountability is an attitude which builds the habit of keeping our word, taking responsibility for our lives, and honoring our obligations. If you are willing to make this commitment, and take full charge of your own life, it will bring you many benefits!

In a society which is inundated with mediocrity, including attitudes of non-accountability, those all-too-few individuals who meet a higher standard... will be noticed and respected! *Others will be attracted to you, will want to work with you and for you, will want to help you, **because <u>you</u> are predictably accountable... and most of your competition is not!***

Those who are men and women of their word, who do what they say they'll do, who honor their responsibilities, and admit when they've erred, are the men and women who will rise like cream to the top!

"Good thoughts and actions can never produce bad results; bad thoughts and actions can never produce good results." (James Allen; *As a Man Thinketh*)

CHAPTER SEVEN
STUCK IN THE RUT... OF YOUR "COMFORT ZONE"?

They were an average family, living in a typical middle-class neighborhood. Both spouses worked, and together they enjoyed an average income and lifestyle, although they weren't saving for college, crises, and retirement like they preferred. They usually had neither the time nor the money to do many of the things they loved to do. Despite this, both believed they were doing as well as most of the people they knew. He was impassive about his work. The pay was 'OK,' but the work very routine. She genuinely liked her job, though the pay was low. All-in-all, life seemed good. The husband had a friend who wanted him to join in a potentially lucrative business, and they had spent a great deal of time discussing it over the past two years. Despite his trust and admiration for their friend, and being convinced that the opportunity had some merit, the husband just couldn't convince himself that he needed to do more.

In another city, a middle-aged professional had it made, by most standards! He had a relatively successful practice, a growing family, and an upper-class lifestyle. Twice a year, he and his wife went on romantic getaways. The rest of the time, though, he worked long hours and often felt burned out. He wanted to spend more time with his wife and children, but his profession was too demanding. In recent years, his health had started to suffer. Knowing that a chronic ailment could soon force him to quit his practice, he pushed himself to maintain the lifestyle they were accustomed to. They were making good money, but spending most of it on lifestyle and the children. Despite his health concerns, the professional chose to ignore opportunities to diversify and leverage his income. He just didn't want to make any changes, right now.

Like the above examples, most of us have a comfort zone. As the name implies, we become comfortable with where we perceive ourselves to be. While we all desire the better things in life, including comfort, for ourselves and our families, we face a potential trap if we allow an *impression of adequacy and success* to place and keep us "in the rut"!

What's a "Comfort Zone"?

The comfort zone is hard to quantify, because it will vary with the individual. My comfort zone will be different from yours. It has more to do with a feeling, than with an actual set of circumstances, and may be easier to understand if we look at it from that perspective.

When a person has settled into his or her comfort zone, their present circumstances in life feel adequate and secure. Like all emotions, these feelings can be misleading and may cause us to make poor decisions. In the comfort zone, one will believe and say things like: "we're doing OK"; "we're doing the same as everyone else I know"; "we're better off than most"; "I'm just not interested in changing anything, right now"; and the classic: "we're broke, but we're happy!" Essentially, the total of our conditions leaves us feeling more or less content, and not motivated to change anything!

The comfort zone is governed by the status quo! Regardless of the individual's true conditions, there is not an incentive to change or improve anything. They have become comfortable right where things are. Nothing seems so bad, that it needs to be fixed!

There is a hidden danger, though, lying within this place! For many, feeling comfortable with life is a goal they've strived to achieve. Once reached, it is very easy to think that we've attained success, and there's nothing more to strive for. Believing this, we tend to put our lives on autopilot, and look to just coast and cruise until retirement, and beyond. Our focus is on maintaining what we have, rather than continuing to achieve, grow, and become more. *Is there a better way to describe that condition of life we may call "mediocrity"?*

What we are describing and defining, then, is the willingness to just be average! As just another average person, family, doctor, lawyer, truck driver, employee, we are stuck somewhere between great and poor, for our particular educational and occupational background. If we don't have the good life, but we aren't destitute, then we must be getting by. By definition, most Americans are doing OK, getting by, just being average. But, have you thought what average means, in the context of society? A great description is: *"the best of the worst, and the worst of the best." This is where our comfort zone is!*

Complacency is the ruler... in the comfort zone!

Average isn't so bad! What's the problem?

We must consider the premise that average isn't so bad! Chapter one shows what average America has become. Average equates with mediocrity, or worse, when evaluated over our lifetimes. For any occupation or profession, there is also an average, which defines the best of the worst, and the worst of the best, within that occupation. Even the highly paid professional can compare himself to the average for his profession. Regardless of what we do for a living, being average does not necessarily make one successful, in the long term.

Professionals are frequently no better off, entering their later years, than are typical non-professionals. A million-dollar mortgage, on a fixed and inadequate retirement income, is no less frustrating than a hundred-thousand-dollar mortgage, on a fixed and inadequate retirement income. A poor marriage is no happier, with a higher income, than it is with a low one. The wealthy stroke victim suffers like the poor one does. We're still broke or miserable, just at a different level! I found myself unable to live in the lifestyle that I wanted, following a successful career as a military officer. I felt like a failure, at first, until I realized that none of my friends who retired from the military were doing any better. <u>All</u> were re-employed. <u>None</u> able to retire!

Secondly, great human achievements, discoveries, inventions, works, come from people who operate **outside** their comfort zone! There is a popular Kenny Loggins song, *Danger Zone*, which was the theme of the movie, *Top Gun*. Both the song and the movie portray that excellence in worthwhile goals comes only to those who think and perform in their danger zone (i.e., beyond their comfort zone!). Think of the accomplishments which inspire you... didn't they result from someone's willingness to risk, stretch their limits, and accept a challenge? Columbus took tremendous personal risks in order to discover the New World. Our earliest settlers put it all on the line, when they uprooted their families for life in a strange and untamed land. The Wright brothers went against conventional wisdom, and subjected themselves to ridicule, by their conviction that a machine could fly. In every Space Shuttle are men and women who risk their lives for science, discovery, knowledge. *Think how little we would have if all people stayed only in their comfort zones!*

Even more relevant to you, are you now, and will you always be, truly content living only within your zone of comfort? There is a human need to feel important, and significant. In all likelihood, that need will remain unsatisfied while living without challenge and risk! Besides this, even our basic needs for shelter, food, love, may not be met without daring to do more. It is not uncommon for plans to go astray, jobs to be lost, investments to lose money, crises to occur. *Can we ever be absolutely certain that we have it made?*

Without doing more, can you guarantee your spouse and children that you'll always be able to care for them properly? Will your family be able to survive a long-term injury or illness? Will you be able to enjoy a financially independent retirement? Living without risk and challenge is to assume that we will never desire more from our lives, than what we have right now. Sitting in our comfort zone, and striving only to maintain what we have, is as illogical as being one point ahead at halftime of a game, and stalling for the entire second half, hoping the other team won't score. Life, itself, is a gamble.

Striving only for certainty, can, at best, still not assure us of keeping what we have. **It will, however, almost guarantee that we will never have more!**

How'd I get stuck in this rut?

If you agree that vegetating in the comfort zone isn't wise, what causes us to take root there in the first place? In a nutshell, *we are lulled into the complacency of the comfort zone by a lack of motivation to go beyond it.* This can result from a number of things. Most of us are unmotivated because we have no goals, no vision for doing and becoming more. This situation may be found in those who have enjoyed enough relative success to believe they are doing 'OK.' Without dreams of a better life than we have at present, none of us will have the ambition to push beyond our comfort level. For others, fear or hopelessness may also hold us back. We may not have a financial vehicle that we believe in. Distractions, such as sports, video games, and the internet, can sidetrack us and become misguided priorities. The average American watches so much television that over 40 hours of life passes them by every week.

Another trap is being hung-up on security. A later chapter addresses this potential pitfall. For now, suffice it to say that placing too much emphasis on perceived security of our circumstances, and on doing nothing which seems insecure, is a sure way to become entrenched solidly in a rut! And, never move forward.

Finally, there are just some among us for whom the comfort zone is their goal. This is the assembly who will, at best, just do what they're doing, and hopefully get by their entire lives. For those in this category, unemployment compensation, social security, medicare, medicaid, and other social service entitlements are probably major elements in their financial planning.

How do I get out of it?

We must be ***motivated*** if we are to break the shackles of the comfort zone. Motivation comes from two elements. One element is <u>want, need, or desire</u>. Our vision, dreams, and goals are crucial to driving us beyond the things we find comfortable. Unless we have something that we sincerely and passionately want to accomplish or achieve, we will have no ambition to do more than we're doing. The second element is <u>belief</u> that we can have what we want. We must have investigated, analyzed, and studied our means, methods, and abilities for obtaining what we desire, sufficiently to convince ourselves that we have a winning plan and vehicle. *Believing we can achieve our dreams gives us the force which will move us beyond the comfort zone.*

If the comfort zone is about mediocrity or being merely average, within the scope of our lives, then what is required to move beyond? This answer is self-evident: it first requires that we ***think differently*** than the average think! The average person is firmly entrenched in their comfort zone, unwilling to risk, unwilling to challenge themselves, unwilling to do what they find distasteful. It stands to reason that, if we want to be better than average, you and I will need to do what they are unwilling to do. This means we must face the reality of risk.

All investors are familiar with financial risk-taking. Low income investments involve low-risk options, such as bonds. The higher earning potential, though, always comes with higher risk. In life, our most valued qualities also involve ***risk!*** Love makes us risk vulnerability, intimacy, the pain of potential loss. A strong spiritual life requires time, study, thought, communication, and effort, making us subject to criticism and ridicule. Financial independence is achieved by being driven, focused, determined, persistent, sometimes almost ruthlessly devoted to our goals... often resulting in criticism and condemnation by those who don't understand.

Investors must decide what they want, then determine what

they must risk to get it. The same is true of life! Trying to stay risk-free, in the perceived security of our comfort zone, is the same as burying our money in the backyard, rather than attempting to leverage it in a bank or investment. Our money may seem safe in the backyard, but it's guaranteed to cost us because it can't keep up with inflation. *Our lives may seem secure in the comfort zone, but we will lose ground because the inevitable changes and opportunities of life pass us by.*

We must be ready to accept new challenges and tasks, even those we don't particularly relish! Every occupation, profession, or worthwhile endeavor has certain aspects and requirements that most of us don't like doing. Many of us don't like dealing with people, yet, nearly all successful people have had to learn to do so. The successful athlete or performer must endure the pain and boredom of years of practice. To have above-average lives, in any area, *we must often do the opposite of what the average people do.*

The average person only wants the jobs that have little to do with other people, and that involve limited responsibility. You and I can excel by seeking the opportunities which involve people and responsibility. The average man only wants to do the minimum to just keep his job. This allows you to go the extra mile, and be noticed for the best positions. The average person devotes little or no time to self improvement and growth, content to just stay as they are. Another may reach superior goals and achievements through personal development efforts. We could go on and on, but, hopefully, the point is clear that to be better than average... **we must do more, and differently, than the average do!**

Albert E. N. Gray, a 30-year official of Prudential Life Insurance Company of America, wrote a pamphlet entitled *The Common Denominator of Success*. In this classic and inspiring document, Mr. Gray says: *"The secret of success of every man who has ever been successful... lies in the fact that he formed the habit of doing things that failures don't like to do."*

"No one would have crossed the ocean if he could have gotten off the ship in the storm." (Charles F. Kettering)

"The only peace, the only security, is in fulfillment." (Henry Miller)

"The enemy of the best is not the worst, but the good enough." (L. P. Jacks)

CHAPTER EIGHT
REAPING THE NEGATIVE RESULTS OF A NEGATIVE ATTITUDE?

Their friend had just left after spending the afternoon watching football. He's a very intelligent guy, a former professional, and one of the best in his field. He has a very nice family, and one of the nicest homes in their area. To look at how they lived, you'd assume this man had to be happy. You'd be wrong! Just a couple years earlier, he had to retire prematurely from a profession he loved. Since then, his age prevented him from entering those occupations that he wanted. His attitude took a nose-dive. Anymore, he complains about everything from the government to the weather. Being around him was depressing. Even though he could be a good friend, people began looking for ways to avoid him.

Perhaps, you know someone like this man? Negative attitudes are not hard to find in the world today. Sometimes, it seems that nearly everyone is! In this chapter, we'll investigate how negative attitudes affect us, and keep us from reaping a more satisfying life.

Just what is a Negative Attitude?

We may recognize this attitude in others, when exposed and sensitive to it. Webster's dictionary defines "negative" as "opposite to or lacking in that which is positive." Also, they say it is "the point of view that opposes the positive." If a positive person generally has a *constructive and affirmative* attitude, then a negative attitude generally is *destructive and contradictory.* A positive attitude is *hopeful, sees possibilities, oriented toward the future.* The negative thinker, however, *perceives hopelessness, impossibilities, and lives in the past:* what "could'a, should'a, would'a, might'a, ought'a," been. Since we're talking about an overall <u>attitude</u>, this aura of *negativity permeates nearly every aspect of one's life, from the way they feel in the morning to how they deal with people.*

It is important to understand that we are discussing a general attitude of negativity, and not just isolated instances of disagreement! The fact is, our very nature is part positive, part negative. *When in proper ratio*, these two sides of our nature keep us out of trouble, yet moving forward in life. The negative and skeptic in us causes us to look before we leap, investigate before we act, consider alternatives, think things through, and so forth. Without healthy skepticism, we could be gullible, and, in the words of a popular country song: "you'll fall for anything!"

Skepticism is only healthy in an open-minded thinker! Only when combined with a willingness to get the facts before making judgments, can we benefit from any skepticism. Combine skepticism with closed-mindedness, and you have a person who is trapped in the prison of their mind... critical of everything, unwilling to investigate, going nowhere!

So, what might be considered healthy skepticism, versus being too negative? While impossible to exactly define, let us think of our minds as a whole pie. If we were to cut our pie into eight equal pieces, no more than one piece should be negative, the other seven should be positive. One piece is sufficient for sensing the potential pitfalls inherent in life's choices. Unless the other seven are possibility oriented, success oriented, "can-do" oriented, forward thinking, positive slices... *the arguments "against" will stalemate the arguments "for," by creating doubt.*

By its very nature, doubt is a powerful enemy of progress! Doubt leads to the *paralysis of analysis* and *defeat by indecision.* If we allow skepticism and doubt to gain strength, indecisiveness gives way to a growing expectation of hopelessness and failure!

The evidence is all around us. Listen to other people as they discuss life's challenges. The easiest position to take and defend is always the negative one! We don't even have to be knowledgeable in a subject to argue against it. In contrast, one must usually know something about the subject to argue in favor of it. You will also notice that it is much easier to change someone's mind toward a negative viewpoint, than toward the positive. Let your friend come to you, excitedly, about a great new opportunity he discovered, and in just a few minutes with only a few questioning and contradictory comments, you can send him on his way, dejected and deflated. If you and I can so easily dissuade another from their positive aspirations, how much more easily may our cynicism squash our own hopes and dreams?

With this perspective, then, any negativity in excess of 'healthy skepticism' becomes a negative attitude. To protect our minds from this condition, we must constantly insure that we have a strongly dominant positive outlook. *When healthy skepticism is counter-balanced by a dominant positive nature, the result should be good, sound decision-making, that is progressive, not regressive.* But, if the skeptic, cynic, and critic in us gains too much control, beware! We are on the road leading to mediocrity, or worse!

The negative in us believes that nearly everything and everyone are useless, and that few things are possible! Should negative thinking begin to grow, it creates a mental atmosphere of doubt, fear, worry, indecision and stagnation. Even worse, if this cynical state of mind becomes dominant, we place a dark cloud over our entire existence. *Our tendency is to only look for and see the worst in virtually every issue and person.*

How did I become so Negative?

We live in a world which will, at best, always have a negative side. Bad things happen. We are going to be exposed to less than positive things in everyday living. For a variety of reasons, we are becoming a society which is out of balance in this attitude! We are subjected to an over-abundance of dissenting and critical viewpoints, in our workplaces, homes, and socially. Many trends present increasing challenges and problems for people, and they're often frustrated, angry, critical and very vocal about them. The constant criticism, complaining, and condemnation by others has a seductive effect on us... if we allow it. Too often, we join the chorus!

Perhaps, you're a lead singer in this negative chorus! Life isn't always fair. Things don't always go our way. Often, it may seem like the deck is stacked against us. This is especially true as society gets increasingly complex. And, it's even truer when there are so many trends going the wrong way. It's too easy to feel frustrated, and maybe even angry, if we perceive ourselves to be stagnating or going backward, rather than making progress. Unless we recognize the futility in getting down, we risk falling into a woe-is-me attitude.

Far too many of our everyday influences are negative! Seldom do movies, videos, or television send upbeat, uplifting, motivating, and positive messages. Death, infidelity, immorality and destruction are what sell and get ratings... so that's what we're shown, day after day, night after night. The news is focused on what went wrong, who got hurt, who and how many were killed, whose doing something bad to whom. Video games portray violence and destruction. Many publications have similar themes. Even the computer and the internet can expose us to the darker sides of human nature. The real culprit, though, is the television set... because we absorb its negative messages, hour upon hour, every single day! This constant bombardment of negative will dominate our will and our attitude, unless we consciously avoid it whenever possible!

Some of us are both blessed, and cursed, with family members or close friends who have fallen prey to negative thinking. When we are frequently exposed to such attitudes, in those otherwise good people that we care about, whose attitude will dominate? By observation, we can conclude that a negative personality usually overpowers those who have less than a very dominant positive attitude. If true, then this is a serious pitfall for those who wish to walk a positive path. We, who are parents, know that a "bad kid" can drag our sons and daughters down the wrong paths. However, we sometimes don't recognize that, even as adults, our own minds can be pulled down a path of negative thinking by the poor attitudes of those we spend our time with!

When we total this array of influences, which bombard our minds and attitudes on a daily basis, it is not hard to see why you and I may become overly skeptical and cynical! As we sink deeper into negative thinking, *we focus more and more upon what's wrong, what we don't have, what we don't want, who we dislike... and we forget and ignore the blessings in our lives, the things that are right, friends and loved ones, and what we want for our future!*

What Negative Results am I Reaping?

Every person knows that when they plant corn seeds, they get corn. If they plant onion seeds, they harvest onions. They recognize a law of nature that says you reap what you sow. Not only is this a natural law, but it is a biblical and a success principle! We will reap a harvest of lifetime achievements and happiness based directly upon the seeds of thought, attitude, preparation and effort that we plant! If we continually sow seeds of negativity, flowing from a negative attitude, we will ultimately reap negative results of unhappiness, discontentment, and under-achievement.

A negative attitude sets a vicious circle in motion! As described earlier, a mind weak in positive thinking is easily neutralized by doubt, fear, worry, cynicism, and indecision. Doubt and indecision lead to missed opportunities, good things don't materialize, and failures occur. With every new disappointment, the attitudes of cynicism and skepticism are reinforced, and become more ingrained. Thus, we are on the 'slippery slope,' falling deeper into the pit of under-achievement and frustration: living lives of quiet (or vocal) desperation!

Words reflect our thoughts, feelings, attitude, and habits. From a negative mouth comes "can't, won't, couldn't, shouldn't, wouldn't, impossible, won't work, no good, I quit," and the other words and phrases which say "no" to people, ideas, and opportunities. These words support reasons not to, rather than reasons to, take action. Without action, nothing changes and no worthwhile accomplishment occurs. All of our greatest failure habits are directly or indirectly related to a negative attitude, mirrored and reinforced by our own words.

Unlike a magnet, opposites do not attract, where state of mind is concerned. Negative people like to be around other negative people, because they can feed off each other's woes, hangups, and injustices, thereby feeling that someone understands and approves of their own downtrodden life. Positive people, on the other hand, generally have little patience with those who are negative. The positive man or woman will go out of their way to avoid one who is negative. If a negative individual receives only negative advice and support, which is oriented toward *inaction*, how can they change? Those people who are positive about life are the ones who could most help, but are the very ones avoided and repelled. Therefore, our negative attitudes serve to trap us, by driving away the positive influences of those who might have helped us move forward!

A negative attitude will cause us to tread water or sink, not swim to shore. By its very nature, this attitude is oriented toward "impossibility" and "can't do" thinking. Nearly all of us would like to have better lives, do more things, go more places. Holding us back, though, are those worries, fears, and doubts that we can actually do more. Regardless of the person, their background, education, and capabilities, an attitude dominated by negative thinking will prevent that individual from taking positive action. They will never reach their shore!

Such an attitude often causes us to give up and not finish what we start! Even when we find the courage to take the plunge forward in some way, a negative attitude can hijack us. It's still there, waiting for the inevitable setbacks and challenges to make us pause and worry. And, once we hit those stumbling blocks, as we invariably do, negative thinking raises, like the genie from the bottle, every doubt, fear, worry, and skeptical thought we ever had. Unless we're truly committed and determined, the genie of negativity only has to raise our self-doubt to the level of indecision... and quitting. He wins again! One more winner... has become a loser.

Negativity is an attitude habit, not an absolute. Attitudes, like all habits, can be changed by the force of our will. We ultimately control our own attitudes! Our negative attitude is influenced by self talk. We can ingrain conscious negative thoughts firmly into our subconscious mind, by continual repetition. Over time, a negative attitude can become a powerful and deeply ingrained habit and can be increasingly difficult to break. The longer we wait, the harder it's going to be to overcome, the more it holds us back, and the more damage it inflicts!

The end results of a negative attitude are never good! Sowing and nurturing the seeds of doubt, fear, and impossibility-thinking, serves to neutralize our mechanisms for taking positive action. It prevents us from receiving the advice and counsel we need. It paralyzes our decision-making ability. It becomes a habit which influences our every thought, word, and deed. The harvest we reap is one of stagnation and frustration, losing ground in the game of life!

What do I need to do to change?

The first step in moving toward a positive attitude, is to understand the value of doing so. Make sure you fully comprehend why ***all worthwhile achievements can only come from positive thinking.***

Discover, again, what you really want out of life! Dare to dream of the kind of person you want to be, the things you want to have and do, and what you desire to give back to humanity. *Unless you can **develop a dream** of a brighter future, and keep it foremost in your thoughts, you'll not be*

68

motivated to change.

Internalize and emotionalize the positive thoughts of what you want. Write down your goals and dreams, surround yourself with anything that reminds you of them, and repeat them often and with conviction, daily. Any time you notice negative thoughts entering your mind, consciously replace them with thoughts of a positive nature, including reading your dreams and goals.

Form the habit of possibility-thinking, by focusing upon why you should, why you can, how you will; look for the good rather than the bad, whatever the issue. Concentrate your mental energy on why <u>to</u> do something, instead of why <u>not to</u> do it.

Create positive inputs in your life! Start a lifetime habit of motivational, inspirational, and personal growth reading, every day. The bibliography lists recommended books which would be a great place to start. Develop friendships with people who have the kind of life and attitude you want to have. Avoid those people who tend to pull you down, not lift you up.

Nothing of value will come from negative thinking! Only the positive side of your nature is oriented toward accomplishment, success, and happiness. Develop your positive self... and live your life as you really want to!

"I was always complaining about the ruts in the road until I realized that the ruts are the road." (Unknown)

"Many of life's failures are men who did not realize how close they were to success when they gave up." (Thomas Edison)

CHAPTER NINE
HANGING OUT... WITH SOUR GRAPES?

The woman was recently divorced, and starting life as a single mother with a teenage daughter. She was a good lady, ambitious and eager to make her way in the world, with dreams of great accomplishments. However, very shortly after getting her new apartment, she became involved with a group of people who frequented one of the area's popular bars. Needing support and friendship, she quickly became a regular at their particular hangout. Soon, her outlook and goals began to change. Once determined to achieve big things, the lady now began to settle for choices involving low paying jobs. Her talk changed to subjects of partying, drinking, who drank the most, and who ended up with whom. Within a year, her teenage daughter became pregnant and left home for a time. Those who had known the mother for years shook their heads sadly, as they watched these changes take place, seemingly powerless to alter their course.

Another fellow, Ken, was a college graduate and a former collegiate athlete. Still single, he moved to a small community and sought to find permanent work in the recreational or counseling fields. At one time, he exhibited genuine enthusiasm for moving on in life. However, he found solace and friendship with those who had little or no ambition. In the comfort of lounge nightlife, he molded relationships with those who spent their time there. Within months, Ken lowered his sights to doing odd jobs and living in a beat-up old apartment. Gone was his desire to enter the professional world of counseling, for which he had trained. No longer did he talk of owning a recreational facility one day. The old Ken had been swallowed up by a new and unmotivated one.

Many parents know too well the effect that a *bad crowd* can have on their sons and daughters! Some of us sense the need to protect our children from the poor influences of certain individuals. Few of us, unfortunately, ever consider the effects which similar negative associations have on us as adults. In the following sections, we'll make you aware of how potentially damaging this pitfall can be; and how it can derail your future.

Negative Association... spending time with those who pull us down!

Association, as we are discussing it, is defined as: "the fellowship or friendly partnership with those individuals who have similar ideas, interests, and purposes." Another definition, in our context, is "those who we voluntarily spend our time with." Contrast this with some of the relationships at our places of work, which may not be voluntary nor go beyond the workplace.

*Our chosen associations become negative if those we associate with have qualities and influence which **dampen our ambition and cause us to sink to or remain at lower levels of achievement.*** These alliances are seductive and deceptive, because they feel like friendship and they satisfy our need to belong. We can feel contentment with people who are actually holding us back, and we often rationalize such relationships because they seem friendly, supportive, receptive, and accepting.

The *Power of Association* is a principle alluded to in other chapters, and is discussed in our religious worship and by success authors and speakers. Throughout the ages, it has been noted that *we become like those we hang around with.* An excellent place to study this principle is at the typical bar, watching those who meet regularly to drink and have fun. However, negative associations may be found at our work, socially, or within other organizations! We may have negative relationships with our spouses or children, among teachers and other professionals, and with members of our families. *Any person or group with whom you have a relationship which tends to **pull you down** rather than lift you up, is an association whose influence can reduce your potential.*

71

Why Do We Associate with other People?

You and I have a basic need to feel like "somebody"! From adolescence, our ego and self-esteem are in a constant state of development and change. As humans, we are naturally gregarious, and much of our self worth is based upon how we fit in with those around us. When we feel loved, wanted, accepted, approved of, and so forth, our self-esteem is high. If other people disapprove of us and reject us, however, we no longer feel important, and our self-esteem and happiness sink to the floor. To feel good about ourselves and who we are, we need to be wanted and accepted by other people.

The ultimate feeling of importance is when another person genuinely loves us! The emotion of love brings a high degree of acceptance and approval, but carries its greatest weight because someone else cares deeply about us and wants to be with us. They want us for who we are. This feeling is only better if shared mutually with the same person.

Few people ever love us in the way described above. In the absence of such love, or outside of love we have, our ego still needs to be nurtured. This is where most of our informal associations come into play. We become involved, and continue, in such relationships because we find satisfaction in being "one of the guys." In all such associations, we are seeking to satisfy our basic need for *acceptance.*

We associate voluntarily with other people and groups *to feel important.* To achieve this feeling of importance, we must have a relatively high degree of agreement and commonality with those we are spending our time with. Being around people who think like we do, who share similar ideals and goals, who generally approve of our thoughts, words and actions, heightens our self-esteem and ego. Our tendency is to seek conformity! Only when members of our informal associations conform generally to the same standards do we have the complete sense of togetherness and approval that all members are after.

Observe voluntary associations between people, and you'll see the tendency toward conformity, homogeneity, and similarity. In the military lifestyle, where I spent over 20 years of my life, our off-duty relationships were usually with those of *similar interests*. Officers generally spent their time with officers, enlisted with other enlisted. The "ground-pounders" got together for their various parties, and the pilots flocked to their typical "watering hole" to discuss flying. Military doctors, engineers, and attorneys, had their own support groups, apart from the rest of us. The same tendencies exist among civilian groups, such as teachers, blue-collar workers, and other professionals. Whatever our vision is of ourselves, we tend to adopt the perceived values and qualities of our associates.

Another underlying reason for association is the *need to belong*, as to a family. This is perhaps a common thread within those street families we know as gangs. When children, or even adults, have a limited sense of belonging at home, they will often search for acceptance in organizations outside the home. For many of our nation's children, gangs satisfy the need to belong, as well as offering acceptance and approval.

We may sum up the varied reasons behind our associations with the common sense wisdom: *birds of a feather flock together!* Whatever may drive each individual, we spend our time with those we consider to be like us (birds of our feather). Just as nature segregates its species, for the most part, so too do we flock together with those we relate to the most. Crows fly around with crows; middle income attorneys hang around with other middle-class attorneys. Blackbirds form large groups with other blackbirds; lower-income wage-earners spend time with other low-income blue-collar types. While deer band together with other deer; we invite fellow fans to our homes to cheer for our football team, and don't usually invite supporters of the other team. *Birds of a feather flock together... because they feel a sense of importance, belonging, and acceptance from having perceived values, ideas, words, and actions in common with those around them.*

Why Does Poor Association Hold Us Back?

Now that we know something about why we associate with others, and about negative association in general, let's consider how it is that certain associations prevent us from going forward with our lives.

As we concluded earlier, *birds of a feather flock together...* ***even when the birds share a bond of mediocrity!*** Therein lies the problem. Far too often, the most alluring associations are those which involve people who like to have fun. While there is nothing wrong with having good clean fun once in a while, many such relationships involve little except the pursuit of a good time. In those associations which typically hold us back, mediocrity is the accepted lifestyle, and the usual goal is seeking pleasure or gaining recognition.

Negative relationships attract the lowest common denominator! We discussed the tendency of our associations to pull us toward conformity and similarity. This follows the human need to be recognized, receive approval, and feel important. Each individual member feels the same pull to succumb to the group's ideals of thought, words, and actions. In relationships which pull us down and hold us back, the core values of the group or individual are based on mediocre and less-than-positive qualities. The subtle and not-so-subtle pull is always toward those core values.

There is a quirk of human nature that makes us envy or even dislike those who achieve more than we have, especially if we know we could be doing more than we are. Rather than cheer for the winner, or the guy or gal with ambition, we tend to put them down and belittle their goals and achievements. Perhaps we feel threatened by those who seem to be like us, but who achieve more than we're accomplishing. Whatever the reasons, *negative associations will discourage us from doing more and going further in life than those we associate with.* Mediocre friends do not want us to succeed beyond mediocrity. If we try, we will meet immediate resistance. The harder we try to change, the more they will attempt to keep us where we are.

Profound examples of the power of negative association may be discovered among groups like gangs, bullies, and extremist organizations based on racism or hatred. However, we can have detrimental relationships with people in generally accepted groups, such as bowling and other sports groups, in our churches, and so on. No matter what purpose our associations may have, the pressure is to conform! *In less-than-positive relationships, we are expected to sink to the others' standards.*

A dramatic example of the power of association can be found in looking back to Germany prior to and during World War II. Hitler developed the personal charisma and dynamic personality to convince an entire nation that a race of people should be exterminated. Despite the knowledge that such thinking was flawed and evil, hundreds of thousands were swayed by the persuasion of one man to sink to the level of committing unthinkable atrocities involving torture, murder, and genocide. Nazi Germany demonstrates the power that association with the wrong thinking can have upon our lives and the lives of others.

Should you have the ambition and motivation to want to become more, do more, have more, give more, you will have to consider the effects of your associations... and consider changing some.

How Should We Associate?

Birds of a feather... flock together! This adage, simple as it is, gives us the answer. Just as negative associations tend to pull us to the lowest common characteristics, and hold us there; *positive associations can uplift, motivate, and inspire us to achieve more of our potential. **The key is whom we choose to develop relationships with!***

You are obviously one who wants to do more with your life, or you probably wouldn't be reading this book. Since that is the case, *you will need to purposely develop relationships with those individuals and groups who possess the knowledge, qualities, wisdom, occupation, education, skills, or lifestyle... that you want!* Once you find them, these are the people who have the greatest possibility of influencing you to achieve and become what you want. It is with men and women of this category, where you will find the most positive association.

In *The Master Key to Riches*, Napoleon Hill devotes considerable discussion to analyzing the "Mastermind Principle". He says: *"Realizing that one may find in almost every group of associates some person whose influence and cooperation may be helpful, the man of keen discrimination, who has a Definite Major Purpose he desires to attain, will prove his wisdom by forming friendships with those who can be, and who are willing to become, mutually beneficial to him. The others he will tactfully avoid."*

Virtually every reputable author on the subject of success, tells us time and again of the *value of forming friendly alliances (positive associations)* so that we may have mutually rewarding and helpful relationships... relationships which help us progress, not regress.

Unless we want to spend our lives scratching the ground with turkeys... we had better learn to associate and fly with the eagles!

Losers can't stand winners... they will always try to pull a winner down!

Mediocrity is a powerful magnet... those who want better lives are wise to avoid getting too close to its advocates!

CHAPTER TEN
BLINDED... BY LACK OF VISION?

Janet was a small town girl. She was talented, with a likable personality and obvious potential. But, she seemed to never accomplish much. Her marriage to a construction worker was lackluster, at best, and they struggled from payday to payday, never having much left over. She brought in some supplemental income as a babysitter, and on occasional odd jobs. Once, Janet had a chance to make a new and potentially lucrative career decision, but she quickly lost interest. She just didn't seem to see herself doing or having more. Her life continued to be very routine and mediocre. She spent most of her time concerned with relatively insignificant things, fretting about the minor issues, ignoring the major ones.

Tommy's grandparents and parents had all worked in the timber industry, and they expected Tommy to follow. Times had been hard, though, and there had been a definite downturn in the industry. Tommy was bright and outgoing, and could have done just about anything. However, he did not consider doing anything outside the timber business. Years later, after struggling to make a living, he was heavily in debt and his personal life was a mess. Still, he remained in the industry that he knew, blind to other options that might have been better.

These, and countless other examples, show the long-term devastation we do to our lives from not daring to dream how much more we could do and be. While other factors may also play a role, the one we will study is that of vision, or, more appropriately, lack of vision. Unless you and I have some greater vision of what we might do, what we might become, we trap ourselves in our present circumstances.

What Is "VISION"?

Vision is best defined as "a mental image," but could

secondarily be defined as "the ability to foresee something as through mental acuteness." Specifically, we are talking about your vision of the person you are capable of becoming; the contributions you can make to the world by virtue of what you do and how you live your life... *your dreams of what you can be, have, do, and give!*

If you like athletics, you probably know that many great athletes and teams have honed the ability to see and feel victory before they've achieved it. This is vision. Sports psychologists make a living in part by helping their athletes develop this skill of visualization. Olympic high-jump champion, Dwight Stone, would stand at his approach, and visualize every step leading to and through the clearing of the bar. Sometimes, his visualization would take several minutes, as he first saw himself making the jump before he actually did it. The United States women's ice hockey team, during the 1998 Winter Olympics, visualized not only their spectacular play, but even the gold medals being placed around their necks. They created these positive images days before they actually received the gold medal. These athletes were mentally seeing themselves doing that which resulted in success. Most of us, in our everyday lives, overlook the power of vision in shaping and guiding our future.

Vision has played a part in virtually every human accomplishment since time began! Try to find even one house, one bridge, one skyscraper, one monument, one marriage, one child, that did not find its beginnings in the mind of the creators. Every significant human achievement must be conceived in the thoughts of someone, before it takes form. James Allen says, in *As A Man Thinketh*: "... dreams are the seedlings of realities." Your mental images, of what you hope to achieve, include your dreams. Our dreams are our "fondest hopes." As we dream of our greatest desires and hoped-for achievements, we create a vision, or mental image, of those events, times, or places. Having mental images of our fondest hopes, our dreams, we can establish goals which will take us step by step toward attainment of those dreams.

Goals are the thought and planning tools that we use to achieve our mental images. Goals are the building blocks of our lives. Goals can also be visualized. If my vision is to live in a peaceful country setting, my dream might be a beautiful colonial home, and one of my goals could be the purchase of the land upon which to build that home.

"Vision," then, is our mental imaging of what we truly and passionately want to become, do, have, and give as a result of being on this earth.

Why Do We Lack "Vision"?

There is no simple answer to this question. One reason is lack of knowledge... **ignorance**. Very few people teach us the value of having vision, dreams, and goals.

My Grandpa Burgess used to say "If you're going to dream, dream big, it doesn't cost any more!" Although he died when I was a small child, I had the benefit of his words as my Dad repeated them. However, nobody else offered me similar advice, not even the schools I attended. Most of us receive the opposite advice. What we hear most often is advice such as "be realistic!"; "stop your daydreaming, it'll get you nowhere!"; "don't expect much, and you'll never be disappointed!"; and "get a good education and a good job, and everything will work out OK!" Many times, such advice comes even from those who love us, our own parents and families! Seldom do we hear differently from our teachers. As a society, we are being indoctrinated to not dream, to not establish a vision for our life, to be **ignorant** of our potential.

Expectations of parents, family, and teachers can prevent us from developing our own unique image, or vision, of what we may become. In many occupations, such as ranching, there is a tradition to uphold. Frequently, the expectations of family bind the youth to the family tradition, even if the young adult is more suited to something else. The same is true within other occupations, from timber workers and heavy equipment operators to doctors and lawyers. Teachers may also have their own expectations of us and influence us in those directions.

Similarly, **low expectations** can produce chronic under-achievers. For various reasons, usually well-intentioned, parents may set low standards for some or all of their children. This may also occur in our marriages and in our workplace. Low expectations can become so ingrained in us that we become lazy, hopeless, and dependent, perhaps for our lifetime. With no motivation to improve, many of us become adults with literally no vision for being anything close to our true capability. Without a major intervening factor or crisis to break the grip of complacency, we will probably amount to almost nothing, compared to what we might have been.

Contributing to the problem of low expectations, is the fact that almost **none of us know what our full potential is!** The limitations of the human body seem to be reached by each generation, yet surpassed by those who follow. No Olympics passes without new world records in at least some events. Every year, new athletes reach levels of performance that previously seemed impossible. No one can say just how much farther we will push the boundaries of physical capability. Yet, the capacity of our minds is even greater!

Scientists do not know the full potential of the human mind, and can only make educated guesses. Even the most optimistic guess, though, has us currently using about 10 percent of our mental capacity. If this is accurate, then *you and I live our entire lives without tapping 90 percent of our brain's capability.* If you reflect on this, the implications are staggering! Consider all the magnificent creations and achievements in our human world, so far, using just 10 percent of our brainpower. How much more can we accomplish, if we could just double that? By setting low standards and expectations for ourselves, or for those we influence, and not daring to challenge our limits, we fail to come close to our full human potential! This ignorance is mirrored by our attitude toward our abilities.

As we mature and age, too many of us acquire an **attitude** of just settling for whatever we get out of life. While the reasons are varied, the result is predictably consistent: *a fatalistic acceptance of mediocrity!* Without a vision or dream of accomplishing and becoming more, we turn our lives over to luck, chance, and circumstance, absolving ourselves of responsibility for what we are or will become.

Where Do We Go... when Blind to any Vision?

"As a man thinketh in his heart, so is he," writes James Allen. He, and wise men and women throughout the centuries, promote the wisdom that we are what we think. And, we become the sum total of our thoughts, as time goes by. In my Grandpa's wisdom, "dream big, it doesn't cost any more!", hide two great truths. One truth is that dreaming big is the only way to become greater than we are at present. The other is that dreaming small costs us dearly in terms of **lost potential!** The vast majority of the human race envisions themselves far below their real potential, and *since they must first think it in order to achieve it, they never come close to their greatest and best use of their lives.*

Napoleon Hill, in *The Master Key To Riches*, says: "It is one of the great tragedies of civilization that ninety-eight out of every one-hundred persons go all the way through life without ever coming within sight of anything that even approximates definiteness of a major purpose." Hill spent over twenty years of his life studying the most successful people in America, and he concluded that having a definite major purpose (or a vision) for one's life, is essential for the attainment of worthwhile objectives in that life. He also says: "It is no less impressive to observe that those who are classified as failures have no such purpose, but go around and around, like a ship without a rudder, coming back always empty-handed, to their starting point."

The Bible tells us that "man without vision shall perish." Isn't it telling us that a man or woman without goals, dreams, a

81

mental image of living fully... *is not living as God intended us to live?* The body may be alive, simply going through the routine of existing, while the mind vegetates and life passes. When we cease to envision becoming more, when we stop dreaming of greater achievements, when we have no goals... aren't we almost in a self-induced coma? Without vision and purpose... are we really living?

It has been my lifelong observation, and too frequently my own personal experience, that nearly all of us **think too small!** The rancher could build a beautiful home for his family, but instead builds a shed for his cattle. The ditchdigger has the ability to operate the largest earthmover, yet he labors at the end of a shovel his entire life. The doctor or lawyer has the intelligence and aptitude to create great wealth and share much-needed knowledge with the world, and they lose it to a lifetime of stress and tension, focusing only on their day to day challenges. *Few of us dare to dream of what we could do, have, be, and give, if we only set our sights higher!*

Have you ever set a goal, and didn't make it? If you're like me, it happens all the time. In fact, I very seldom hit my goals exactly as I planned them. However, I come closer to them than I would have with no goals at all! And, so do you! Dreams and goals, if they're worthy, stretch the limits of our perceived capability. Just like an Olympic athlete, who has her aim on a world record, *our goals should challenge us. If they don't, they probably aren't worth achieving.* It makes sense, then, that great and worthwhile goals will sometimes, if not most of the time, be set back or knocked off course, and we'll come up short. Keep this in mind, and consider the effect of having low or no dreams or goals.

Since we seldom hit our goals exactly, what happens when we have very low goals, or no vision for achieving much of anything? Chances are, we don't hit even those low aspirations on the mark, either. Life just happens, and sometimes we get knocked off course, regardless of how slow the course was. So, *even when we set our sights far below our potential, we are likely to miss even that target.* If you and I aim for an upper-class lifestyle, we are very apt to get hung up in a medium income bracket, at least for a time. If we set sail for an average life of just getting by, we could very well spend some time in both the unemployment and welfare lines. Can you even imagine where we'd be, living an entire life with <u>no</u> goals, dreams, or vision?

The average person would never consider starting a vacation without at least a map and a plan. Yet, the typical person will embark on a lifelong journey of work and living, without ever preparing a plan for how he or she wants to progress. *Lacking a definite major purpose, a vision, we wander through life as if floating in the middle of a river, allowing it to take us where it will.* Without direction, we have turned our lives over to pure chance, luck and circumstance. Then, when we get stuck or overturned on the inevitable rocks, sandbars, and tree trunks, or permanently hung up in a brushy bend, we howl to the world about the injustices we've suffered. *Rarely do we stop to recognize that if we had a vision, a dream, a plan, and goals to guide us and give us a sense of direction, a purpose for living and becoming, we would have minimized the dangers and increased our chances of succeeding!*

How Do We Take the Blinders Off?

Observe the most successful men and women that you know. Carefully study how they think and act. Chances are, you'll get a lesson in **goal-setting.** Chances are, you'll see people who constantly envision doing more and greater things than what they've already done. In their minds' eye, they see an image of what they could still become as they continue to dream and create goals.

The first thing you and I need to be acutely aware of is the importance of creating a mental map, an image, a vision, of what we want our life to represent. Unless we can see in our mind the vision of our **definite purpose** for living, we'll just wander willy-nilly through life, accomplishing little. If you were to die tonight, how would you want the obituary in tomorrow's paper to read? It should tell the living why and how you lived. This is the vision you should have of your path through this world!

Then, dare to **dream!** If we become what we think, then our fondest hopes, our dreams, should represent the very best that we're presently capable of becoming and doing. Dare to dream that you can go beyond your present circumstances, that you can become the person you know is inside you, waiting to surface. Envision the realities you want, for yourself and for those who depend on you. Dare to dream, and teach your children to dream! James Allen wrote:

The dreamers are the saviors of the world....Dream lofty dreams, and as you dream, so shall you become....The greatest achievement was at first and for a time a dream. The oak sleeps in the acorn; the bird waits in the egg; and in the highest vision of the soul a waking angel stirs. Dreams are the seedlings of realities.

See what could be, not what is! Be aware of your boundless potential, and don't be dismayed that you are not there yet. Nature has always required a maturation process for all its living things, and you and I are no different. The mighty Redwood trees of California and Oregon are centuries old, and reach hundreds of feet into the sky. Yet, they did not become mighty overnight, and when they started from tiny seedlings, who could have guessed what they would become? Even the native, who walked among them as mere one-hundred-year-olds, might have vastly underestimated their future growth. *See what you could be, not what you are!*

In *The Magic of Thinking Big*, David J. Schwartz writes this:

...the deeper I dug into what's really behind success, the clearer was the answer. Case history after case history proved that the size of bank accounts, the size of happiness accounts, and the size of one's general satisfaction account is dependent

on the size of one's thinking. There is magic in thinking big.

In the United States of America, it is nearly impossible to <u>not</u> make a living. With our great resources, systems, and limitless opportunities, all of us are capable of getting by. You'd almost have to <u>try to fail</u>, to not get by in this great country. Therefore, don't be afraid to aim higher than just getting by or making a living. Doing this is just average. You have more potential than just average; don't be reluctant to **set higher expectations for yourself**. Visualize what you could become, have, do, and give... *if you just try!*

As my Grandfather said: "Dream big, it doesn't cost any more!" (But remember: dreaming small can yield a lifetime of lost achievement, low productivity, and unhappiness!).

Here lies a person who exited the world without knowing why he entered it. (Inscription on a gravestone.)

CHAPTER ELEVEN
SUCKED INTO THE CULT OF CONFORMITY?

Joe was debating whether to go into the family business with his Father, or go to work at the local factory. Just out of Junior College, he considered himself to be very independent. As he considered what to do, though, numerous friends kept downplaying the responsibilities of business, and playing up their perceived advantages in working for someone else. Finally, he decided to get a job at the factory, and assure himself of a regular paycheck.

During his first day on the job, Joe met with his Union Steward. The Steward explained to him the various advantages of union membership and procedures. When Joe asked about moving up within the ranks by virtue of exceptional performance, the Steward stopped him cold. "You have to understand," the Steward warned, "that standards have to be the same for everyone in this organization. If any member does more than the job description calls for, the company will start to expect us all to do it. We can't have that situation, so you absolutely must not do more than your job requires!" Joe got the message, and from the first day, he did only what he was expected to do, no more.

Joe did, however, notice what he thought was an inefficient way to perform one task. He began to experiment with a possibly better alternative. While engrossed in this effort, his general manager observed his different procedure. He quickly jumped all over Joe, and said in no uncertain terms "We do it this way around here, not another way. Take your pick, it's either our way... or the highway"! Joe never again tried to look for any alternative to the company way.

Can you relate to any of these examples? Have you ever felt like your individuality and creativity were being squashed, that you were expected to conform to the standards of other people, whether you really wanted to or not? This may be more common than many of us realize. And, it may prevent us from advancing in life, if we allow it. Together, let's shed some light on the concept of being "sucked into the cult of conformity"!

When Is "Conformity" a "Cult"?

Conformity is simply defined as "similarity," or "conventional behavior." When you and I conform to a set of standards, principles, or types of behavior, we are adopting a set of guidelines usually developed by someone else. In many cases, behavioral guidelines are beneficial for the common good, such as with our laws. To create an orderly society where all people have the greatest relative freedom, we must have generally accepted standards of conduct to insure that one person cannot usurp the freedoms of another. Under such a lawful and organized governmental system, we are obligated to conform to the standards (laws) established for the protection of all. To this extent, similar and conventional behavior (conformity) is a good thing. It helps assure our basic freedoms and way of life!

Informal expectations for behavior, however, of a specific group of people, may or may not be such a good thing! In this chapter, we are going to consider those situations when conformity may not be beneficial to us, in the long run. We hinted at some of those situations in the above examples. Other instances could involve such things as following trends in clothing worn by a particular group. If you have sons or daughters, you are probably well aware of the pressures children are under to wear the "in" clothing, right down to the same kinds and colors of sneakers. Similarly, many of our youth adopt a smoking habit, despite the widespread knowledge of the dangers. There is no more logical reason for this persistent trend, than the need to conform to the in-crowd's idea of grown-up behavior. We adults, also, tend to conform to the expectations of some of those around us, even when it may not be in our best interests.

The conformity that we need to zero in on is that which can be detrimental to us! It is this prospect that leads to the matter of "cult" behavior. Cult is literally defined as "devoted attachment to a person, principle, etc."; or "a group of people having a common set of beliefs." In this strict definition, a cult may be a very innocent thing. Given this interpretation, even Christians, Jews, and Moslems are involved in cults. The same with football fanatics, car salesmen, motorcycle clubs, hunters, fishermen, bridge club players, and so on. However, in our society the concept of cult has taken on a generally negative or even sinister association.

Mention the word "cult," and most of us conjure images such as Jim Jones, who had such a magnetic attraction (maybe reinforced with a bit of force) on his followers that nearly one-thousand followed him in mass suicide. Or, the 1997 case of 28 people following their fanatic leader to death in the belief that a comet would whisk their souls to a better world. For our purposes, let's take a moderate interpretation of the word, and let's think of a cult as *a group of people having a common set of beliefs, or who are devoted to principles... **which are probably not in our best interests!***

Given the above concepts, then, *"conformity" becomes a "cult" when you or I voluntarily accept and behave according to the beliefs or principles of a group of people... although doing so is probably not in our best interests!*

With this common reference, we can now think about those instances when we may be conforming to the potentially damaging standards of other people. We've already mentioned how this situation affects our youngsters when they feel compelled to smoke, like their peers are doing. Likewise, experts believe that most children are sexually active by the end of their high school years. For the majority of our youngsters, sex is probably highly influenced by peer pressure... the need to conform to behavior that is apt to be detrimental to their healthy development. As adults, you and I are influenced by various groups, as well.

There are many formal and informal groupings within our

complex society, whose members share in and conform to various beliefs and principles. We've mentioned labor unions as being one such formal group, where members are encouraged and sometimes even pressured into conformity. There is a principle of success referred to as going the extra mile, doing more than you're expected to do. In organizations which discourage members from doing more than they are paid to do, members are denied use of this proven principle for bettering one's life. In this example, those who conform are doing so against their own long-term best interests.

A nation's military could be considered a cult of conformity, also, because members certainly are expected to behave in ways that are often detrimental to their own life and interest. In many aspects, though, the military cult is meeting higher standards which benefit society as a whole. Throughout history, men and women have always sacrificed for a higher cause. Some expected behavior, however, may be negative and cult-like. For example, during much of my military career, you were expected to work hard and play hard. Play hard was generally defined as "drinking hard at the club." Drinking hard produced unfortunate results, such as violent or adulterous conduct, drunken driving, downgraded performance, accidents, and so forth, which were not acceptable. Yet, there was pressure to conform, and be considered a team player. Other professions and occupations have their own cult-like standards of behavior, as well.

Teaching is an honorable profession! Teachers work hard, put up with much, and are seldom paid what they are worth. However, I have observed that the teaching profession also has its own unspoken values which members seem to willingly conform to, despite the fact that they may be harmful to their own success. Since teachers are experts within their own particular field of study, they tend to develop a closed-minded attitude toward opinions, ideas, suggestions, and opportunities which run counter to their way of thinking.

Teachers are generally employees, hired to do a job. Perhaps for that reason, I also observe a pattern of discrimination among the teaching profession toward business. In several years association with junior and senior high schools, not once did I witness even one teacher encouraging a student to consider going into business. Seldom have I met a teacher who would consider going into business. Within the teaching profession there appears to be a conformity of attitude which promotes job-ism and discourages free enterprise. Yet, capitalism and business are what created and still drive this great nation! Even our teachers fall prey to conformity.

Society has its own set of standards and principles which we knowingly or unknowingly conform to. You and I frequently place too much emphasis upon the opinions and expectations of others, considering that most will not stand up under close scrutiny. Often, we call this unwritten standard "conventional wisdom," though wise it may not be. For one example, examine our general expectations from our own government. A great number of us blame the government for our woes, demanding more and more programs to make it right. Few of us reflect on the fact that we the people created, run, and finance our government. We seem to have the attitude that "they" owe us... more and more and more. Many of us accept this, without challenge, and conform to the ideals of those who believe that none of us should be responsible for our own lives... the government should be. This attitude is driving us straight into socialism at a high rate of speed!

We've already touched on the attitude of "job-ism." It is not only teachers who generally conform to this principle, but society as a whole! Our government leaders talk 99 percent "jobs" and one percent "business." Ask one-hundred of your neighbors what they would do for a living, and at least 95 of them will tell you "get a job." For those who don't want a job right now, the next choice is "get a better education, so we can find a better job." Jobs have their place and serve a purpose within a free enterprise economy, and many of us do need the job vehicle as a stepping stone... but, jobs are not the end all, be all.

Most of the highly successful men and women used the business vehicle, primarily. Surveys show that about 99 percent of all US millionaires are in business for themselves! Over 80 percent of them have less than a college degree of education. About 95 percent of the working population are employees, while less than 5 percent ever become financially independent. It is a society-wide myth, perpetuated by conventional wisdom and conformity, that getting a good education and a good job are the only way to succeed. And, most of us buy it without challenge or second thought!

Conformity also tells us to get a divorce from our spouse if things aren't going well. If it isn't right, get another one! If you demand proof, watch television and read the newspapers. Our national divorce rate exceeds 50 percent. We try on spouses like we try on shoes, except most of us would spend more time with the shoes. Divorce has become so common that it is almost in vogue to either have one or be in the process of getting one. Yet, we leave a trail of broken hearts and disheartened children scattered along the path! Meanwhile, counselors and relationship experts tell us that the majority of marriages could be saved if both people only made a genuine effort to do so. Obviously, we are conforming to the standard of those who tell us "end it at the first sign of trouble." Sucked into the cult of conformity!

Great People... Think Differently!

Consider those men and women who, throughout history, have had the most significant impact upon their fellow man. You will find that nearly all went against the grain of conventional thought and standards of their day. Study great people, from this perspective, and you'll discover that non-conformity is almost a prerequisite for greatness!

Christopher Columbus totally defied those who believed that the world was flat, as he dared to discover the New World. Many considered him to be a complete lunatic, but he didn't worry about what they thought. Henry Ford invented a horseless carriage during an era when the horse drawn vehicle was king of the road. He had non-believers and critics, but he didn't let them stop him. Orville and Wilbur Wright were considered "nuts" when they tried to build a machine that would fly. Their own Father even tried to stop them. They persisted, anyway. Benjamin Franklin had his critics, yet he challenged many of society's beliefs to become one of our greatest inventors.

William Wallace, Scotland folk-hero, refused to conform to British rule. Today, his courage is given tribute in the academy-award winning movie, *Braveheart*. In 1877, the great leader of the Nez Perce, Chief Joseph, refused to conform to the onrushing tide of white expansion and domination. Only when his people finally faced total destruction did this brave warrior yield and make his historic speech "... I will fight no more forever." His determination and bravery are remembered to this day. Martin Luther King provided a calm, non-violent, and inspiring message at a time when racial hatred and violence were orders of the day. His rock-solid stand and the unshakable quality of his values changed the nature of race relations in America, forever.

In more modern times, we have our heroes, also, who refuse to conform to the belief standards of someone else! In India, Mother Theresa refused to join those who looked the other way, she saw the plight of the poor and did something to make a difference. England's Princess Diana, Princess of Wales, had a worldwide impact because she would not conform to the past standards of "royal" thought and behavior. Bill Gates dared to compete in the volatile computer industry, and became the wealthiest person in the world during the 1990's. He didn't even attend college.

The US had never had a female Cabinet-level Secretary, but in 1997 Madeline Albright challenged that standard and became Secretary of State. At a time when it's still not fashionable to demonstrate religious faith, following the 1998 Orange Bowl football game, players from the University of

Tennessee and the University of Nebraska huddled at mid-field. Holding hands and kneeling, they gave prayers of thanks before a national television audience. These young adults were not afraid to show the rest of us how to perform mightily while maintaining humility. *We can all learn much from such examples of positive non-conformity!*

Great men and women do think differently! Observe carefully, and think deeply, about this concept. Understand that we are <u>not</u> talking about outlandish behavior and attitude, which is more the result of rebellion, greed, selfishness, and immaturity than from independent thinking. There are many negative examples of non-conformists who are anything but a positive role model! Rock stars who engage in offensive behavior, spitting blood, throwing excrement, etc., are certainly going against conventional behavior, but are hardly who we should want to emulate. Murderers, such as Ted Bundy, Jeff Dahmer, and other criminals, don't conform to society's standards of decency. This kind of behavior is both self-destructive and unpardonable within any lawful society. Hitler was a brilliant thinker and non-conformist, but he ignored universal standards of human decency and internationally accepted law, and that made him bad. We are not talking about these kinds of self-aggrandizing non-conformity. We are talking about having a mind of our own, having a set of worthy values, and being an independent thinker!

The people who affect others dramatically, in positive and uplifting ways, are people who have the logic, maturity, and courage to do their own thinking. These people seek the advice and counsel of only those whose knowledge they respect, they study the works of experts to gain knowledge, but they don't worry about other opinions and expectations. Independent thinkers have always challenged old ideas, standards, and methods. Men and women with the courage to follow their dreams, convictions, and values have always been the trail-blazers, the pioneers, the adventurers... the heroes. Conventional wisdom says "do it this way because that's how we've always done it." Independent thinkers are willing to look for the better ways, yet unknown and unaccepted. *All human progress has been the result of independent thinking and the courage to defy "common knowledge" and conformist beliefs.*

Independent thinkers, who affect humanity in the most positive ways, are people of moral value and conviction! It's always easier to do wrong than to do right. The mass of humanity tends to take the easy way out, when given a choice between right and wrong. Perhaps we don't do entirely wrong, but we may not do entirely right, either. *The man or woman who truly evaluates, logically, the differences and advantages of having moral values, will choose to have them! It is moral virtue, combined with the conviction of courage,* which moves the rest of us so greatly, when we are in the presence of such a man or woman.

A recent example demonstrates this entire concept. There is a textile factory named Malden Mills founded in 1865 in Lawrence, Massachusetts. It has been the town's largest employer, and a pillar upon which the community depended. Just before Christmas 1995, a fire totally destroyed Malden Mills. The owner, Aaron Feuerstein, aged 70, was independently wealthy, and could easily have taken the insurance proceeds and walked away from the plant permanently. Every logical business person and employee would have understood if he had done so, but Mr. Feuerstein did not accept conventional standards. Recognizing that many of his 3500 employees had been with his family business 30 to 40 years, or longer, and that they and the entire community depended upon his company tremendously, Aaron Feuerstein continued all payroll at full wages, and started rebuilding. Two years later, every employee was back on the job, and the new plant was in full operation. Mr. Feuerstein is a fabulous example of a man who combined logical, independent thinking with real values, unselfish values, and did what few other people would have done, in similar circumstances! He did not conform to conventional wisdom. *He had the courage to do what he believed was the right thing to do!* ***This is what makes great people... great!***

Dare to Be the Best You!

The essence of this chapter is to encourage you to be an independent thinker. *Virtually all of mankind's lasting and greatest achievements were the product of the mind of someone who could think for himself or herself.* Great accomplishments are the fruits of those brains which dared to challenge the common knowledge and conventional wisdom of the day, or of the group. Not just to be different or controversial, but this kind of person risks criticism and condemnation because they have logically thought through the issues, sought knowledge, studied it, analyzed it, and weighed it against their standards of right and wrong.

I would encourage you to think about your values and principles. Hitler was an independent thinker without a moral foundation based upon the value of human life. All our heinous crimes are committed by non-conformists who have not established moral values for guiding their lives. Values and principles keep us on a path which is constructive, not destructive; one which is positive, not negative; one which benefits ourselves, without taking unjust advantage of another. Independent thought, without morality, creates history's monsters. *Moral values are like the warning signs and guidelines on a highway, they help us stay safely on the right road. Know what you stand for, and live by it!*

Lastly, become a person who has the ***courage to act*** on the strength of your own logic and convictions! Sheep must always be a part of a herd, must always have a group to follow. Far too many of us are like sheep, always following the herd. When we behave and act like the group behaves and acts, we'll reap the same results the rest of the group are reaping. Have the courage to set a better standard for them to follow... the courage to think independently, the wisdom to know the values you want to live by, and the conviction to do what's right, whether the group understands or condones it, or not. In other words, *don't simply be like everyone else you know... be the best YOU!*

Dare to be different... dare to be YOU!

"The greatest pleasure in life is doing what people say you cannot do." (Walter Bagehot)

"The trailblazers in human, academic, scientific, and religious freedom have always been nonconformists. In any cause that concerns the progress of mankind, put your faith in the nonconformist!" (Martin Luther King)

CHAPTER TWELVE
VICTIM... OF A WELFARE MENTALITY?

Jake had two job interviews this week, but he decided against both. They would entail a 20 minute commute, and he just wasn't up for that much driving. Besides, he really didn't want to work anyway, nor did he see a pressing reason to. He was living at home with his parents, though he was in his early thirties. Despite being unemployed for nearly two years, he picked up an occasional odd job and, with his social services check, he got by. It helped that his folks didn't charge him to live at home. It was actually better being unemployed, because his former wife had no real leverage on him to pay child support. And besides, Jake's family had a few bad breaks when he was small, and Jake figured the government owed him. Without a formal education, he could only qualify for lower income jobs, and he wouldn't make much more than he did with unemployment and social services support. So, why bother, he figured!

If you have friends or family who sound similar to Jake, do you sometimes feel that handouts aren't helping? Do you think that maybe we're harming some people by giving them too much, when they're capable of doing more for themselves? If so, this chapter may interest you as we attempt to deal with the "welfare mentality" which is far too prevalent in society today.

We All Need Help Sometimes!

Few of us go through life without having some bad breaks! In severe cases, short-term assistance from family, friends, or the government could be a real lifesaver to help us get back on our feet and going forward again. During the stock market crash and the Great Depression, in the first half of the 20th century, people lost their entire life savings, many also lost their jobs, and great numbers found themselves in soup and bread lines just trying to survive. Much of the unemployment compensation and social services systems we have today resulted from experiences during this cataclysmic period in our history. In the beginning, these programs were created to fill a real and perceived need for a safety net system to prevent the mass suffering such an event could trigger in the future.

Our current systems are a product of change and refinements to the original safety net. When used as intended, they are a huge benefit for those participants who run into hard times for reasons beyond their control. Used as designed, these programs provide much needed relief while the down-and-out person has a chance to weigh his or her options and seek better and permanent solutions. The man or woman who temporarily is unable to find employment, or who needs financial assistance during a period of great crisis, should feel no shame in accepting such assistance. That's why it was created, to provide help when major crises strike.

Likewise, most families need to assist certain members at various times. Some of our youth need the financial support of grandparents to help fund education expenses. Newly married couples may require some guidance and help getting started in their life together. As couples age, their children have occasionally been expected to support their parents emotionally, physically, and financially, to varying degrees. Such inter-family dynamics may not always be welcomed, but are relatively common in larger families. It's just a fact of life that some individuals will need financial or other help at certain times. *For those who do, there should be no lasting remorse when, despite our best efforts, it just hasn't went right!*

The "Welfare Mentality"... and How It Hurts Us!

In this discussion, we are <u>not</u> dealing with those legitimate instances when otherwise productive people are in need of temporary governmental or other assistance. Such men and women will accept help graciously and thankfully, and <u>end the need as quickly as they can</u> by establishing a new option and plan for themselves. These individuals have too much pride and self-reliance to accept help from any source longer than absolutely necessary. They are very different from those individuals and cases this chapter was written to address.

A person who has the welfare mentality, is generally one who believes in or promotes the concept of "something for nothing." This kind of thinker can rationalize that they are <u>owed</u> the help, that it is not a privilege but a right. One with such an attitude will overlook the fact that assistance isn't free, but comes from somebody else's pocketbook. *Once a person convinces themselves that someone else, including the government, owes them, they no longer accept responsibility for their own lives. Therein lies the essence of this problem!*

The Damage from Receiving More Help Than We Need or Deserve!

The United States of America was founded on the principle of economic and personal freedom! In such a free nation, the citizens have a high degree of freedom and choice to determine their own destiny. Citizens may pursue their dreams using all legal means, coupled with ambition, courage, and persistence, to rise to whatever heights they are willing to work for. With complete economic freedom comes the necessity of taking risks. Risk always means that we might not succeed. And, freedom to choose and risk requires that failure be an ever-present companion for our system to remain truly free. Individually, temporary failures are valuable learning experiences which can both increase our knowledge and build our character. When we don't allow an individual to fail, if he deserves to fail, we deny them opportunities to learn and grow into stronger citizens. *As a nation, without the freedom to take chances, to risk failure, and to overcome the consequences, we no longer have a free economic system... we become a socialist system where the government controls our destiny!*

The inherent danger, for a free society, in having governmental safety nets such as our welfare and unemployment systems, is that they may be abused by those who will milk them for more than they were intended to provide! Historically, such programs have too little effective oversight, and it has been far too easy to take advantage of them. In effect, especially for those who abuse the system, such supports cushion our individual failures. *Reduce the consequences of poor decisions and incorrect actions, and we fail to learn from our mistakes, we aren't compelled to make better future choices, and we do not mold our character in the forge of adversity.* In the long run, we may weaken our citizenry by taking away their right to fail, lessening the value of their decision-making, and making them dependent upon others and less reliant on themselves!

When any individual is given more help, especially financial, than they need or deserve, a damaging dependency is created. Since our welfare system is designed only to dole out, not take in, such aid is "free" to the individual concerned. They are not required nor expected to repay any of the assistance they receive. Therefore, undeserved aid quickly becomes "something for nothing"! The dependency begins the minute a recipient starts to perceive aid in that light.

As governmental or family assistance becomes "something for nothing" to an individual, we begin to reward all the wrong values in that person! Rather than rewarding such qualities as ambition, wisdom, persistence, hard work, education, and self-reliance, undeserved assistance instead rewards values such as laziness, fear, doubt, selfishness, quitting, giving up, sometimes even dishonesty, and so on. The person who would willingly accept more help than is truly needed, sacrifices their dignity, their independence, and their self-esteem for the sake of an "easy buck." Increasingly dependent upon the system (or their family) for their existence, this individual starts to believe the system owes them. Instead of looking to their own individual creativity and efforts for a solution, they look to the system to provide answers for them.

When any of us believes we are owed a living, without having to work for it, assistance has gone too far! With such an attitude, a person has turned control of their own life over to someone else. Refusing to accept responsibility for themselves, they become a leach upon society, always taking but never giving back, and they have essentially destroyed whatever potential they had to become a worthy and productive citizen.

When Giving Hurts!

The issue of the welfare mentality is not just about <u>taking</u> more than is deserved or needed. It also includes those of us who are too quick to provide <u>handouts</u> to the supposed needy! One may have a welfare mentality, even if they've never accepted a dime of help from anyone. We become a part of this problem if we foster the problem in someone else! *Giving more help to someone than they need or deserve, is also part and parcel of the welfare mentality.*

Government comes immediately to mind as we view this challenge from the perspective of giving too much. While many government programs were created with the best of intentions, to meet legitimate needs, over time they tend to grow far beyond the original intent. Combine this with another trait of government, lack of effective oversight, and we create systems which become economic monsters, taking on a self-serving life of their own. The Internal Revenue Service and the Department of Agriculture are prime examples. So, also is the Department of Health and Human Services. The US Department of Health and Human Services reported that total public welfare expenditures, in 1990, exceeded one-trillion dollars. This amount represented over 19% of the Gross Domestic Product of the United States! This nation now spends far more for social services, than it does on national defense.

Most would agree that our welfare system needs immediate reform. At this time, both the federal government and many states are seeking positive ways to reduce and control the various programs within this system. Several states have placed arbitrary limits upon how long a person may draw welfare assistance. The nationwide call for reforms is an admission that the federal welfare system has went too far, and must somehow be reigned in! We must find a way to bring such programs closer to the original intent... to help the truly needy, without becoming a way of life. Such changes are necessary, in the best interests of all concerned, and should be applauded.

Part of the governmental welfare problem stems from the ease with which people may enroll for assistance. We advertise in the local papers, and place flyers in the Post Offices, encouraging participation in various programs. Then, once on a program, there are virtually no controls to insure that aid only responds to legitimate need. Far too many participants are allowed to draw benefits almost indefinitely. We have created a system which almost encourages abuses!

Ordinary citizens are often part of the welfare mentality problem, as well. Many of us throw our money and possessions at those we perceive to be in need, without knowing where and how our aid is used. Panhandlers bilk us for millions every year, playing upon our sympathies and good intentions. In addition, we occasionally promote dependency within our own families, by giving some members, especially our children, too much help. *Whether done out of love, out of pity, or out of charity and good will... giving too much can have very negative results!*

For whatever reason, giving more than a recipient needs or deserves is potentially harmful. We may create a sense of worthlessness and dependency in an individual which lowers their ego, self-esteem and confidence to the point that they become incapable of standing on their own. Some may react by becoming despondent and unmotivated to do anything for themselves. Others may take the attitude that "you owe me" and "you are responsible for taking care of me." Believing that the world owes them a living, they direct their ambitions toward taking every possible advantage of the system or giver. The individual who falls into either trap, risks his potential to amount to anything of value as a citizen.

Give a man a fish, and you feed him for a day! Teach a man to fish, and he can feed himself for a lifetime!

No Matter Who... "Something for Nothing" is Seldom Good!

So far, we've discussed the dangers of excessive giving as it pertains to individuals. We can also create the same dependency and other negative traits in an organization, if we give it more than it deserves or needs.

We have what amounts to a Corporate Welfare System in the United States, as well as an individual one. On the corporate level, tax breaks and subsidies are used to bolster certain industries and businesses. As with individuals, when a corporation or industry becomes dependent upon a government subsidy, and concludes that it's owed them, the business sacrifices a part of its integrity and self-reliance. Instead of looking for alternatives, or better and more efficient ways to perform, corporate welfare encourages the recipient to stay as they are, and make up any deficiency by fighting for more and more handouts (breaks and subsidies).

Likewise, state governments receive federal funding for numerous programs. Even this funding can have similarities to welfare. States can become hooked on federal funds, and rationalize that they are owed them, to the point that dependency can also destroy potential progress. As with individuals and corporations, the states' tendency is to look to more funding, rather than changes in effectiveness and efficiency, as a way to deal with challenges.

Internationally, we have a welfare system, known as "Foreign Aid"! Every year, the United States hands out billions of dollars in aid and uncollected loans to foreign governments. While we have stated goals and motives behind the aid we give to any country, the results of foreign aid can be startlingly similar to those of individual welfare. A foreign nation can not only become dependent upon our assistance, but it can start to expect and demand that aid, as if it is their right. Our controls are seldom any more effective on an international level than a domestic one, and our millions are frequently squandered in ways we never intended nor imagined. As a nation looks more and more to our aid to bail them out, they look less and less to themselves for solutions. It seems that the more a nation believes we owe them, the less progress we make toward our original goals in supporting that nation.

Whether to an individual, an industry, or to a government, giving too much something for nothing in return... usually carries greater potential risks for damage, than for progress!

Experience the Freedom... of Controlling Your Own Life!

This nation was founded upon individual dignity and freedom of the human spirit! No matter how tempting, or needed, aid may be, realize that there is an inherent danger whenever we allow someone to help us, especially financially. Even free aid still carries a high price of servitude for the recipient. This price is paid in dependency, lost dignity, and lowered self-esteem, at the very least. It may cost us lost ambition, lessened motivation, lowered confidence and courage, and destroyed self-reliance. *A major key to accepting aid gracefully and with dignity, is to do everything in our power to get back on our feet and end the aid as soon as humanly possible!*

Nearly every human is born with the ability to take care of himself or herself. For some, it may take more time, creativity, and effort than it will for others. But, most of us have that capacity, if we just look for it until we find it. There is perhaps no humanly concept held in higher esteem than the concept of freedom. Personal and economic freedom unlocks the door to any person's potential, and gives them unlimited opportunity to achieve more and go farther. This freedom produces a drive in the human spirit which is nearly unequaled. And, when a man or woman has overcame challenges and regained control and independence, it is a wonderful feeling!

Recently, an inspiring story came from a small community of Westminster, Maryland. There, a single mother had lost her job, and was facing the prospect of going on welfare in order to survive. Wanting to avoid welfare if she possibly could, she took inventory of her abilities, and decided her talent for baking could be her answer. She began baking muffins in her home kitchen, and with hard work, persistence, and a friendly attitude, she built up a business which paid her way. Then, the health inspector shut her down, for not having an approved commercial baking facility. As news of this situation spread, the local fire department offered the "Muffin Lady" a proposal. If she would provide the fire fighters with morning pastries, she could use their commercial kitchen. Once again in business, the Muffin Lady charged full speed ahead, and she is now one of the most respected residents and business-owners of Westminster... a single mother who looked to her own abilities rather than to welfare! She kept her home, is able to care for her children, and maintained her pride. The Muffin Lady does NOT have the welfare mentality!

Sometimes, we blame luck or past circumstances for our problems. However, luck and circumstances are really the products of how we've lived our lives. The better our education, the more intelligent our decisions, the harder we work, the greater our integrity... the better become our luck and circumstances! So, if we begin to develop these and other positive qualities in ourselves, and take complete charge of our own lives, our circumstances will surely become better in time. If you're one who would like to become more self-reliant, I would suggest a reading program for personal growth as a good way to start.

"People that pay for things never complain. It's the guy you give something to that you can't please." (Will Rogers)

If life gives you a lemon... learn to make lemonade!

CHAPTER THIRTEEN
"HUNG-UP"... ON "SECURITY"?

He was a good man! Paul went to work early, took his lunch so he could eat while working, and stayed late. He did his job well, the same as he'd been doing for over 20 years. He just didn't believe the pending corporate restructuring would exclude him! Confident that his record of performance would keep him on the payroll, or relocate him if necessary, Paul focused on his work and people, turning down several interviews with other local companies. As the day of reckoning approached, Paul was assured that he'd be taken care of. Then, with just a few days before the big changeover, Paul received the word: "we tried, but we just can't keep you on; we're really sorry!" Paul was crushed and stunned. He worked his last days, and began what was to become months of job-hunting and unemployment.

This story is a common theme in corporate America in the 1990's! As global competition and markets change the face, operations, and profitability of business, business has not been "as usual." Today, the job market is a much riskier place to be in. Companies play more reactively to "bottom line" profits, and the frequent reactions are masked by names like; downsizing, rightsizing, rescaling, restructuring, mergers, and buyouts. In this environment "job security" is not what it used to be. Just what is this thing we call "security"? And, how does it affect today's worker if he places too much emphasis on it? We'll examine this issue, and allow you to consider if it might be holding you back?

What do You mean, "Hung-up on Security"?

First, let's agree on what security is, in the context of our livelihood or work. Webster's Dictionary says that security is "a state of feeling free from fear, doubt, care, danger, risk, etc." *It's feeling safe, protected, and safeguarded against unwanted elements.* It is important to note that security can be either a feeling, or, theoretically, an actual condition. In the context of our job, personal, or future security, however, a condition of total security will never exist!

Never can we be 100% guaranteed that either our job or our future are safe and secure for all time. If security could be 100%... we would have a state of utopia. The fact is, you and I will never live and work in a world which has no fear, doubt, cares, danger, or risks. *So, the key point of this definition is that we are talking about a **feeling** of, or a **perception** of, or a **degree** of, <u>not</u> an actual condition of security! Specifically, our focus will primarily be upon the concept of **job security** (occupational security).*

So, how is it that someone can get "hung-up on job security"? To start with, all of us would prefer to have real security, or at least a high degree of it. This is a natural and understandable human desire. The problem occurs, though, when we equate a feeling or perception of security with a state of actual security. Since there is no possibility of ever having total security, especially in our jobs or businesses, *we become unrealistic if we believe that feeling secure is the same as being secure!* We are actually striving for an abstraction, rather than a reality!

We can become fanatical or even obsessed with pursuing or keeping perceived job security. But, since we are dealing with human feeling and abstract perceptions, as much as factual reality, we are subject to error and miscalculation. *We are apt to believe what we want to believe, rather than what the facts might have us believe!* In the pursuit of that ultimate secure job, we can ignore and reject countless potentially golden opportunities, failing to accept that we will not find perfect security. Or, believing that our present occupation is secure, we may pass up more lucrative possibilities, either within or outside of our current employment.

Shouldn't We be Security Conscious?

Obviously, all of us need to be <u>aware</u> of security issues, some more than others. An ambassador to the Ukraine must be much more aware of personal security and safety concerns, than would the ambassador to Canada. A National Football League running back has far less job stability and security, than does a person who works at a bank. The football player could have a career-ending injury in the very next play or game. He could also have a bad year and be cut from the team in a matter of weeks or months. No matter what we do for a living, we should understand and consider the implications of job, personal, and future security. *The answer, then, is that we should be conscious of security!* The question really is: *how much emphasis do we place on it?*

Our view of security relates to how realistic we are. If we understand that we will never have true security, then we can base our plans and decisions on realistic expectations, risks, and assumptions. However, if we are lulled into believing that we can actually have total security, in any aspect of our lives, then our plans and decisions will be based on over-stated expectations. *Plans based on faulty assumptions, are very apt to be the wrong plans!*

Similarly, we also need a reality check with regard to our faith in and emphasis on job security. For example, a professional football player, who realistically knows that his career could be very short for reasons beyond his control, can negotiate his salary, manage his money wisely, set up adequate insurance coverage, and be continuously open to financial options and diversification strategies, in order to prepare for the worst case. In contrast, the same athlete, believing he is secure for a twenty-plus year career, may decide to live a high-profile lifestyle, spending most of what he earns, and be in serious financial trouble, with few good options, should he lose his job the next year.

Some of us have jobs which are personally dangerous. Most of today's workers, though, face as much risk to their income and lifestyle, as to their health and safety. Unfortunately, it can be more difficult to assess lifestyle risk, than risk to our personal safety. It is even more difficult if we don't accurately assess the various trends in the economy!

Corporate America has been going through significant changes for several decades. Many trends drastically reduce the security we used to expect from our employment and occupation. Today's business economy is increasingly global, competitive and cutthroat. Profit margins are often slim, and can fluctuate wildly. Loyalty, of employer to employees, and employees to their employer, can be very low. Profitability is watched so closely by many companies, that decisions become reactive in nature. Numerous tools are used by modern executives to control costs; tools such as downsizing, rightsizing, middle-management restructuring, pension and benefits adjustments, mergers, layoffs, buyouts, and out-sourcing. Employee payroll and benefits are among the largest costs, for the average business. When the going gets tough for any company, these are usually the first costs looked to for reduction. In the final analysis, many businesses simply go out of business. *For the typical employee, his or her job is as insecure as it's ever been!*

Yet, employees continue to place job security very high in their occupational priorities! Many people base their major family decisions on their perception of this one item, as if it were an absolute. This heavy emphasis contradicts the trends referenced above, and seems to ignore the fact that everything in life involves some risk. Accidents, major illness, and untimely death claim and disrupt hundreds of thousands of lives every year. This stuff of life just happens, despite our very best efforts to avoid it. There is absolutely no guarantee that you or I will be physically capable of working, employed, or even alive... one year from now! It is unrealistic to assume that we have, or will ever have, 100% job security!

There are two places on this earth where we can come close to total security! One is in prison. Under the care of the state, a person can live somewhat worry-free and risk-free for a predictable amount of time. The second place is completely secure! There, we are free from the threat of accident, illness, injury and pain. There, we never suffer from criticism or condemnation, threat or accusation. In the quiet solitude of the graveyard, we remain in a state of total security while the grass, flowers and butterflies struggle to exist, six feet above. In the meantime, our decisions should reflect the knowledge that we will never have complete security, especially job security, as long as we live!

How can a "Security Hang-up" Hurt Me?

We can become too concerned with either <u>finding</u> job security, or with <u>keeping</u> it. If we're striving to find that ultimate secure job or occupation, we can place ourselves in a nearly permanent state of unemployment! The reason for this is simple, once we understand it: *A secure job doesn't exist!* Every occupation and job is to some extent insecure. To chase job security is like chasing one's own shadow. We may think we can catch it, but forty years later the illusion is still where it was... just beyond our reach!

When a person chases employment on the primary basis of job security, they may put themselves at a serious disadvantage. Pursuing an abstract quality which can never be perfect, considerable <u>valuable time may be wasted</u>. <u>Good opportunities might be rejected</u>, while looking for the perfect one which doesn't exist. <u>Important experience can be lost</u>, both during the extended inactivity of job-hunting, and because of missed opportunities. Our household <u>income will undoubtedly suffer</u> during extended unemployment. And, worst of all, <u>we fail to prioritize</u> our own individual abilities and responsibility!

Placing job security in top priority downplays our skills, capabilities, and personal responsibility. In effect, it puts the cart ahead of the horse. Instead of recognizing, relying on, and improving our distinctive abilities and potential, thereby assuring our own future wherever we work, we focus on a specific job's perceived qualities. Rather than acknowledge that our skills, abilities, and performance will be our best assurance of long-term security; we look for that assurance in the job itself. *We are looking for an occupation that will "take care of us," when we should accept the fact that "we must take care of ourselves."*

Likewise, the man or woman who tries to keep their job primarily because they believe it to be secure, perhaps because it's a regular paycheck, risks irreversible damage to their financial future! Part of the damage comes from <u>fixating on one financial vehicle</u> (our job), and <u>closing our minds to other options</u>. We tend to <u>ignore opportunities</u> which might enhance or diversify our position. The more secure we feel, the <u>less likely we are to improve our skills and knowledge</u>. Comfortable in our perceived safety, *we focus on keeping what we have, rather than striving to improve upon it.* In the best case, we may remain employed until retirement, then find that our financial assets are inadequate to retire in the lifestyle we hoped for. In the worst case, if circumstances result in unemployment, we may find it impossible to compete with those younger than us or those who have surpassed our knowledge and abilities.

In addition, an unrealistic expectation of job security assumes that we control our working destiny, when in reality <u>someone else does</u>! Even if you're a business owner, you have no guarantee that you'll stay in business. As an employee, your continued employment is dependent on the long-term stability, viability, and approval of your employer. You cannot guarantee that a company will succeed. Market conditions and technological advancements can change a company's profitability almost overnight. Likewise, you cannot control the person who hired you. He who hires, can also fire! Believing we have 100% job security is to assume that only we, not someone else, determine when we leave... this simply isn't true!

Similarly, if we put all our faith in our present occupation's security, we assume that nothing will change! This is contradicted by life itself. Change is one of life's constants. You and I can embrace and manage change, but we will never control it. Therefore, some things will happen which are beyond our ability to influence, and which can alter our plans and expectations for the worse. An automobile accident and a lengthy recovery, or a stroke or heart attack, for instance, can have major repercussions on our family's income and future. *Hinging all our dreams and goals on job security, assuming that nothing will change, is flirting with fire. Sooner or later, we are apt to get burnt!*

Perhaps worst of all, getting hung-up on security places the responsibility for our life (and our family, if we have one) squarely in the hands of our employer! Ironically, we think we control our fate, when we believe we're secure; but, in truth, we've abdicated the right to the boss! Believing we have job security, we think we only have to keep doing what we're doing, and we're assured of staying there as long as we want. We place our complete trust in the employer that nothing will ever change and they'll never consider letting us go. In effect, we think the employer is obligated to employ us for as long as we want to be employed. Nothing could be further from the truth! The reality is this: unless we <u>own</u> the position we occupy, we are only <u>borrowing</u> it from someone else! <u>They</u> determine whether we keep it, or not.

The average American worker places a high emphasis on job security. Yet, according to most financial planning statistics, less than one person in twenty will achieve real financial independence. Nineteen out of twenty will be dead or broke by the age of 65! Nearly 11% of us live in poverty in our old age. Despite the fact that most of us seek job security... are we any farther ahead?

OK, How <u>Can</u> I be Most Secure?

You and I ought to consider job security the same way we consider all other factors in decision-making. We should use logic and common sense applied to an evaluation of the facts. Since total security is a state of utopia which will never exist, then what we should consider is the security risk which we find acceptable. As with any risk, the potential benefits of security planning must be weighed against the possibility of being wrong. Recognizing that no occupation is completely secure, *we are wise to limit the emphasis we place on seeking, or keeping, job security!*

Wiser people than I have said that our **only real security is in our ability to perform and to take care of ourselves!** Accepting complete responsibility for our own lives is a necessary step to hanging up the security hang-up. Once we stop believing that our employer, or our customer, is responsible for keeping us employed, then we are in the proper frame of mind to make sound decisions regarding our future. Then we can realistically work and plan to create our own best and constantly improving life, going forward instead of marching in place.

Recognize that nothing in life is certain, including our occupation or employment! In an uncertain world, it is prudent to have options. Having <u>choices</u>, the ability and willingness to diversify, expand, and improve our position, allows us to <u>hedge</u> against the unexpected. Just as <u>diversification</u> is a commonly accepted strategy for managing money and investments, it is an intelligent consideration where our time and effort are concerned. There are many ways to <u>leverage</u> ourselves more effectively, thereby multiplying our efforts and improving our long-term staying power. These elements could all be part of a winning strategy!

I would suggest that you develop a self-study program as part of a plan for on-going self improvement. Some excellent resources are listed in the bibliography at the end of this book. Create the self-confidence and self-reliance to weather life's storms, and become your own security!

The person who always strives for greater performance, while keeping all reasonable options open, keeping his mind open to new opportunities, and looking for ways to improve, diversify, and leverage his position... is a person with a high likelihood of winning in the game of life!

Why bog ourselves down unduly on job security? Why not learn from the Olympic athletes, accept that winning involves risking, and "go for the gold"?

"Free man is by necessity insecure; thinking man by necessity uncertain." (Erich Fromm)

"Only those means of security are good, are certain, are lasting that depend on yourself and your own vigor." (Niccollo Machiavelli)

"The only real security that a man can have in this world is a reserve of knowledge, experience, and ability." (Henry Ford)

"Only in growth, reform, and change, paradoxically enough, is true security to be found." (Anne Morrow Lindbergh)

CHAPTER FOURTEEN
ARE YOU RIDING A DEAD HORSE?

The old cowboy found himself far out in the pastures, working cattle, when a storm began to brew in the western sky. Knowing he would have a difficult time getting home by dark, he pushed harder and harder to complete his job. His horse was a good one, a pretty mare, but she had been with him all day and was showing a lot of fatigue. Still he pushed, and finally got his cattle where they needed to be, with just two hours before dark and a three-hour ride home. He pointed the mare ranch-ward, and dug in his spurs. She held a hard pace for 30 minutes, then began to quiver uncontrollably as she faltered, shuddered, and fell to her side. Her gasping breath lasted only a few seconds... and she was gone. Later, he found out her heart gave out. For now, his anger and anxiety boiled over! He kicked and whipped the body of his mare, unmercifully, for nearly ten minutes. Finally, fatigued himself, he faced the fact that *he simply was not going to get home... riding a dead horse!*

By now you're probably asking yourself, "what on earth does riding a dead horse have to do with me?" Good question! Let me ask you: are you riding a dead horse where you work? *Is what you're doing for a living, getting you where you want to go in life? If not, you might be riding a dead horse!* In the rest of this chapter, we'll try to make some sense of this concept.

Where is it that You want to go?

The first issue is: *what do you want out of life?* This is a key point to this concept. You see, if we're sitting astride a dead horse, right next to our barn, and our barn is where we want to be... it's no big deal. We can whip him and spur him to our heart's content. Then, we can just step off him and walk to the barn or the house for a cool drink. We're where we wanted to be, anyway. Likewise, if your job was just scaled down by a re-engineering, and you now make half what you were making yesterday, (the horse dies), but you've already saved enough money to retire comfortably in the lifestyle you want... no big deal! In contrast, if your burning passion is to become financially independent by your 40th birthday, but at age 38 you have no savings and your only income is from a minimum wage job... you're going to have a long, slow, and frustrating journey. *It's like trying to ride a three-legged horse in the Kentucky Derby!*

So, just what is it you want to achieve by virtue of what you're doing? If you're like the majority of people today, you probably haven't even thought about that question. This is a part of the problem: *few of us know for certain what we want to accomplish as a result of what we do!*

What is truly important to you? Do you have your aim on an upper-class lifestyle, with a nice newer home in the country? Do you desire to acquire wealth sufficient to allow you to give back through philanthropic organizations, or create one of your own? Do you have family members you want to be able to assist when and if they need financial help, without hurting your own goals and dreams? What are your goals and dreams? Do you dream of a two-month first-class vacation around Europe, or Australia? Or a month-long hunting or fishing or rafting trip in Alaska? How important is your time? Do you want an independent lifestyle? Do you want the time and means to develop a tremendous marriage relationship? Or to be a real presence and influence in the lives of your children? Or, to probe the depths of your spirituality? What do you really, passionately... want as a result of working and living?

An average man or woman might say they want to make a living. But, have you really thought about what it takes to just "make a living" in this great country? The fact is, with such vast resources, opportunities, and social support programs, we're nearly guaranteed to make a living. Likewise, if you want to "get by," you should have little problem! Most people are getting by. This is simply being average in a nation such as the United States.

Perhaps, you want more than that? Maybe your major passion is to achieve a financially independent lifestyle at a relatively young age? All any lifestyle requires is the appropriate mix of money and time. Retirement, at any age, depends only on having the independent income flow to allow you to work or not work as you choose. Some people can retire in their twenties, thirties, and forties. Yet, most of us are brainwashed to automatically think of 65-plus, when the word "retirement" comes up. Would you like to retire by age 50? Or 40? Or 30? With the appropriate income, you could!

As we leave you to ponder such questions, remember these truths. <u>One</u>, *the success of what you do can ONLY be measured against what you wanted to achieve! If you have no idea what you want to accomplish, you don't know if you're succeeding, or not.* <u>Second</u>, *there is a major difference between wishful thinking... and a passionate desire!* ***Know what you passionately desire from life!***

What's Important: the Work? Or, the Results?

Did you talk to a guidance counselor when you were in school? If so, perhaps you received a dose of conventional wisdom! Conventional wisdom usually tells us to focus on what we want to do for a living, our aptitudes, the kind of work we enjoy. Seldom are we asked to consider what results we want to achieve, from doing that work. *Yet, what's most important to you? The **work** that you do? Or, the **results** you can achieve from doing the work?*

Would you work at a service station because you love pumping gasoline? Or, would you work there because the time off and lower responsibility allows you plenty of opportunity for hunting, fishing, wilderness packing, or other interests? Is it the work? Or, the results of the work?

Maybe you're a professional? Are you doing what you do because you so passionately love it that you'd do it even as an unpaid hobby? Or, are you in your profession because it can provide the income and lifestyle that you want for your family? For yourself? Generally, most advice on this subject tells us to find what we're good at, or what we enjoy and want to do... and do that for a living. The assumption is that if we enjoy what we do, we'll be successful. This approach ignores several crucial considerations, however! For one, it doesn't consider whether there is any real demand for what we might do or produce. Maybe that occupation is saturated, and competition would be a major factor. It does not account for the market or economic trends. Perhaps technology is making your selection obsolete.

Likewise, conventional advice doesn't consider the time required to make a living. There are only 24 hours in a day, and our choice may be so time-consuming that, to make a decent income, we'll devote a huge amount of time to the endeavor! If it requires 100 hours of effort per week, is it worth it? Fourthly, conventional wisdom leads us primarily in those directions we're already familiar with, ignoring other opportunities that are waiting for our discovery. Also, *conventional wisdom has us focus on the work that we do, rather than the results that we want from our work! Is that what you want?*

Can **Your** Horse Get You Where **You** **Want** to Go?

Your horse, your financial vehicle, comes in many colors, sizes and temperaments. Financial vehicles are simply those tools we use to create income. For most of us, our vehicle is our job or occupation. Some may have a business which they own and operate. Others, often secondarily, use vehicles such as investments, savings, or a part-time business. Whatever vehicle, or vehicles, we use, nearly all have certain common characteristics which make their potential somewhat predictable.

Generally, we can look at any one financial vehicle, and make a rational prediction of what it's capable of doing for us. The reason we can do this with some accuracy is because jobs pay what the job is worth, not what the employee is worth. Similar products and services, of equivalent quality, must be priced competitively. Also, we are all limited by the number of hours we can work consistently, day in and day out. This is why employees, with about 20 years of experience in a particular industry, generally make very comparable incomes and have the same relative lifestyle. It explains why most professionals, in any specific specialty, will have characteristic homes, cars, recreational interests, and stress levels.

Business owners can leverage themselves considerably, and potentially make very big incomes and reap the resultant lifestyle. For examples, look to Andrew Carnegie, Ross Perot, Sam Walton's family, Bill Gates, Rich Devos, and Jay VanAndel. Some businesses have higher risks than others, and many will lose money and go out of business. Various types of smaller businesses, especially, are quite predictable, with regard to income potential.

Here's a good rule of thumb: if you want to know what kind of lifestyle an occupation may provide, ask the people who are in that occupation. Hear what they say about it. Another rule of thumb: get to know some of those who have done what you're doing or thinking of doing, and see how they live, how content they were with the income and the time demands? What kind of stress do they endure? Do they have good marriages, and are they truly happy? Do some homework! Most occupations are predictable: *if you do what they've done... you'll probably get what they've got! Is that what you want?*

Three-legged Horses... in the Kentucky Derby!

Think about some of those occupations which may have seemed like real thoroughbreds at one time, but later came up lame, or maybe even died. Horses used to pull carts, wagons and buggies back in the 1800's. Those companies that specialized in horse-drawn vehicles could be lucrative investments. Then along came Henry Ford, who dreamed that a horseless carriage could someday carry America down its roads. In just a few years, horsedrawn travel was in decline as the automobile craze took America by storm. Likewise, Orville and Wilbur Wright came up with this silly idea that a machine could fly. Just these two inventions created major changes in the way people traveled, and resulted in a lot of other "horses" going lame or dying!

Technology is driving change at an unbelievable pace! Winning businesses today, can be tomorrow's losers. Thirty years ago, I would have typed these words on a mechanical typewriter. Today, I use a personal computer. Twenty years ago, we jumped out of our cars to phone from a streetside phone booth. Today we call from our cars using cellular phones. Ten years ago, we used the mail to send documents that today we fax and e-mail. Today, real estate agents make good money assisting investors and homebuyers. Tomorrow, will the "information superhighway" make them obsolete... as I place my property for sale on the Internet, and my buyer e-mails his offer!

Are You "Hung-up" on a Bad Horse?

One of the most feared events for a cowboy is to get hung-up on his horse. This happens when the rider is thrown from the animal, but gets his foot caught in the stirrup of the saddle. Out of control and unable to get free from the runaway horse, the rider is in serious and life-threatening trouble. We can also get hung-up on an out-of-control occupation! This can occur when we are putting so much time and effort into what we're doing that we have almost no chance to consider doing anything else that might be better. Often, the less our occupation is providing for us, the more time we put into it (or into two jobs). When excessive effort is still barely allowing us to get by, and we are not progressing toward what we want, we are hung-up on a losing proposition! *We're so busy losing... we have no time to try to win!*

Rearin' to go? Lame? Or Dead?

We're back to the original question: "Will your vehicle get you where you want to go"? By now, I hope you've at least started to think about what you passionately desire to accomplish in life. Since most vehicles, especially jobs, are predictable with regard to their earnings potential, you already have a good idea how you're doing, and going to continue to do, financially. Due to the relentless changes from technological and economic factors, you can assume a bit of risk onto that prediction, depending on what you're doing. *For the results you want... is your horse a thoroughbred? Three-legged? Or, already dead?*

What Is.... IS!!

This seems quite profound, doesn't it? Yet, we tend to forget this fact, especially when it comes to our earning power. Very often, we are extremely optimistic about the money we're going to make! How else do we explain a national per capita credit card debt in excess of $5000? Why are so many of us carrying second mortgages on our homes, if we didn't believe our future funds would cover them? Debt is money we don't have now, but spend now anyway, hoping we'll have the excess money to pay for it in the future. If we just accepted what our income is, and realized it is no more than it is... we'd never spend more than we had; we'd have no debt. Say my income is $40,000 a year. That's what it is. We need $10,000 to buy a used car, but we don't have the money. So, we borrow $10,000, against our future earnings, and we live as if we made $50,000 that year... when we only made $40,000. I am living as if *"what isn't... is"!*

Our occupation is what it is! Everything we do to earn income has a certain potential, and that's what it has, rarely more, often less. Each occupation has other constraints, such as the amount of time or stress required. If I wanted to be a rancher because I romanticize about freedom of time and easy-going, stress-free living, I'd be assuming what normally isn't.

121

While ranching is a great life in many respects, with outdoor work and decent, honorable neighbors, few ranchers have much time freedom. Most are literally married to their work and seldom get away for more than a few hours at any one time. The work requires long hours and high physical demands. Because of extreme market fluctuations, lack of pricing control, plus the ever-present effects of the weather, it's the rare rancher who is unconcerned about money issues. As a result, ranching is seldom easy-going or stress-free. This is what ranching is. It isn't something else. *Your occupation is what it is, also! Will it provide the result you want? It either can... or it can't!* ***If it can't... it won't!***

Perhaps you're thinking we're beating this dead horse to death, about now? Here's why we're stressing this point: *many of us seem to face our futures as if what isn't... is!* The combination of high taxes, rising expenses, and decreasing real income keeps most of us from getting ahead. None of our jobs, nor our health, are guaranteed. We could lose either in the next few days, weeks, or months. Yet, many people have no health insurance; some have no viable retirement plan; and significantly more have inadequate savings. All of us are going to face the day, when we have no choice but to hang up our spurs... and stop working. Health, age, or something else is going to put us there, if we live long enough. Yet, statistically we have over a 95% chance, in modern day America, of being unable to retire with financial dignity. The logical conclusion is that people like you and I <u>don't plan for changes</u> beyond our control and our work. ***Change is inevitable. Yet, we live as if what is... isn't!***

Your financial vehicle, whatever it is, either can... or cannot... fulfill the vision, purpose, and goals (the results) that you want. Most of us go through life kidding ourselves, believing we'll have it all one day, when we are in a vehicle which can't possibly provide the income or which takes too much of our time. Some of us have a lottery winner mentality, living always for the day we're going to win the lottery, never considering other far more realistic options. The challenge to every reader is: *look in the mirror! You either <u>have</u> a definite purpose in life, with a plan and a financial vehicle to help you achieve it.... or you <u>don't</u>!* Do you?

How do I Saddle Up a Winner?

I hope by now you realize that **you have to know where you're headed**... *before you know if you're getting there!* Napoleon Hill says over and over in his books: we need to have a "definite major purpose" if we're ever to achieve anything truly significant with our lives. James Allen says that "Dreamers are the saviors of the world." The Bible says that "man without vision, shall perish." My Grandfather said "If you're going to dream, dream big, it doesn't cost any more." Every highly successful person knows what they want, has a passionate desire for achieving what they want, and they have a plan for getting it. Nearly every person who <u>hasn't</u> achieved all that much... <u>doesn't</u>! How much more evidence do you need?

Knowing what you deeply desire for your life, defy conventional wisdom: don't just look for the easy fork in the road! Have the courage, vision, and the open-mindedness to seek the vehicle, or vehicles, that can take you where you want to go. Anybody can make a living just doing something they want or like to do, or that they're familiar with... and that's about all that most people do. *If you want more than most have... **you've got to do what most don't do!***

Recognize that this world is changing at breakneck speed! Stay flexible and ready to embrace the changes that will undoubtedly come your way, some good, some bad. The winner of today can be the loser of tomorrow. Our best plans don't always work out the way we wanted. Diversity, flexibility, and options are good qualities in nearly all situations, and it's wise to consider them for your life's most sacred plans: your dreams and goals. Nearly every financial planner preaches ***diversification*** with almost a reverence... for good reason. It's a proven winner in the field of finance! *Two horses... take you farther than just one!*

Analyze the most successful and exciting businesses. Look for the hidden ingredient... the secret strategy. When you've finally got to the bottom and sifted it out of the sand of details, you're likely to find it is... *leverage!* J. Paul Getty said it something like this: "I'd rather have one percent of the efforts of 100 men, than 100 percent of the efforts of one man." Leverage allows you to create multiples of your own effort. When we put our dollar into a savings account and get interest, we're leveraging that dollar. If you have a small business and franchise it to ten other entrepreneurs, you leverage yourself through the efforts of ten people. If you can work 25 hours a week, but through alliances with other people you have 1000 hours of effort going toward your business... you have a highly leveraged strategy! The wealthiest man of this decade, Bill Gates, is leveraged every time any computer user, anywhere, buys a Microsoft product. The greatest fortunes and lifestyles of this century... are being achieved by those who understand and use leverage most effectively!

Dare to be informed. Create a regular habit of reading and seeking information. Don't fear knowledge... seek and use it to get where you want to go. *He who cannot find, nor recognize, the best horses... won't get very far, very fast!*

Many great success stories are about men and women who weren't afraid or too proud to start near the bottom. Even at the bottom, real talent and ambition are going to shine. If you haven't attained the vehicle you want, consider starting with one that's at least moving, and continue to work toward the better one. *When the water is too wide, swift and deep... use stepping stones!*

Lastly, *dare to do something!* Only the courage to act, will get us moving on the path to somewhere. *All the best intentions, the greatest dreams, the brightest ideas, and the perfect plans, in the world... are useless in the hands of someone who will not act on them.*

Water seeks the sea, just flowing with the current, always taking the path of least resistance. While the firm resolve of ice... breaks apart mountains!

"*You could have a terrific assignment, your bosses and peers could like you, but if the company's going nowhere, you're going nowhere, and you'd better pick another horse to ride.*" (Kate Wendleton; founder of the "Five O'Clock Club," a career-guidance organization)

CHAPTER FIFTEEN
BARTERING THE PRICE... OF SUCCESS?

Jake had a struggling business and also worked for the National Guard once or twice a week. He had big dreams, and knew he needed to do something more lucrative if he was going to achieve them. An old friend called one day and asked to discuss some ideas they might work together on. Jake agreed, and immediately liked the possibilities! He went to work and started learning new skills. However, Jake wasn't comfortable dealing with people. For months, he avoided this particular challenge. Within a year, Jake was disillusioned because he couldn't get around that one issue. He still knew it was a solid business with the potential he was looking for, but he gave up. He wasn't willing to pay the price it was going to require! He still works at his original business, still not achieving the dreams he had for himself and his family.

Do you know someone who had a great deal of potential in a particular job, business, occupation, sport, relationship, or hobby who just wasn't willing to do everything it took to fully succeed? Perhaps, you, like me, have experienced this yourself, at one time? Does everything have a price? What happens when we try to barter with the price of success?

Everything Has a Price!

Can you think of anything worthwhile, that doesn't cost some amount of time, energy, money, or persistence? *Even the intangibles of life, such as love, good health, a strong and vibrant spirit, our attitude... come with a price.* Certainly, the tangible things, such as food, clothes, our car, home, the education we hope to provide our children, our professional license... all cost us money, at least. Let's think about these costs.

Consider an intangible, one of our most sought after riches, love, having a loving relationship with another person. Achieving a loving and satisfying relationship or marriage requires unselfishness. We must be willing to care, and show that we care by investing time, effort, money, and other resources into the relationship. Many of us must study in order to fully understand our mate, their needs, and how to better meet them. It involves sharing what we do and who we are. We must strive to improve through personal growth, so we can evolve into a person the other can continue to love. It certainly requires the willingness to listen and understand, and the commitment and persistence to keep working at it until we get it right. *This most precious of gifts may be given freely... but, it has a price if we want to keep it!*

Our spirit, attitude, and spirituality, exact a toll, as well, if we are to attain their greatest value. These intangibles of the mind require serious thought and greater personal awareness. Usually we must involve ourselves in a self-study reading program, or perhaps take a few classes at night. We must be committed and willing to persist in a regular program of personal growth. It may require the time and determination to attend religious services and have discussions with others of like mind. We will need the self-discipline to create new habits, and give up old ones. If we are to achieve our mind's maximum potential, we must accept this price!

Good health is another cherished treasure we all seek. While we may be born with a healthy and strong body, we must pay a price if we are to keep it sound and functional. Proper diet and eating habits, diet supplements, exercise, sufficient sleep, and stress management are likely requirements for most of us, if we're to achieve total control of our well being. We have to commit the daily time, effort, and priority to have the best possible physical condition, and then we must be disciplined enough to stick to it, year in and year out. Only consistent and persistent effort will lead us down a path of long-term good health. It's part of the price, if we're to enjoy this body we live in, for a lifetime.

Most of us want a good lifestyle, for ourselves and for our loved ones. *Lifestyle* is that *combination of both time and money* which allows us the *freedom* to achieve those things that are important to us. Nearly all of us must work at some occupation, job, or business in order to create the income or wealth which can give us the freedom we want. This takes our time, effort, and involvement. It also requires commitment, persistence, discipline, integrity, caring, sharing, determination, and the willingness to fail and try again. Our lifestyle depends in large measure on the financial vehicle we are willing to seek, consider, choose, learn, and work at, and what definite major purpose motivates us.

We could continue on and on, with this discussion. Everything from the car you drive, to the food you eat, to the relationship you have with your spouse and children, requires that a mix of time, effort, and personal resources be invested. *Should we attempt to pay less than what they cost, we almost invariably get less than what they are worth!*

Shortcutting... the Shortcut!

A number of years ago, a furor arose in a large Eastern US city when it was discovered that a medical doctor, who had been practicing for quite some time, had gotten his license from a less than legitimate source. He had apparently went to a Caribbean nation, where he found a quick training and licensing program. Then, with his newly acquired license to practice medicine, he set up shop in the United States. Once his credentials came to light, many of his patients sued him for malpractice. The case resulted in new regulations governing licensing.

In another highly publicized case, during the running of a major American marathon, the apparent winner was soon dethroned when officials found out he had cheated. He had left the race route during the first few miles, and worked his way back to near the end of the course. There, during an opportune time, he re-entered the course and proceeded to win. His dishonesty was discovered within a few hours, and the rightful victor was crowned.

Every day, around the globe, we can find examples of someone trying to beat the system, by use of some gimmick, or not doing all they should do. In virtually every business, occupation, and industry one can find those who do less than they are expected to do. Employee malingering, waste of resources, and even outright theft are problems for most major companies. Sometimes, the companies themselves cheat their customers by not delivering the quality or quantity that was promised. Frequently, construction projects are embarrassed, or subjected to legal action, for using substandard materials or practices. Many of us, as individuals, fail to do our work as well and as faithfully as we might have, giving less than the 100 percent of which we were capable. Scandals erupt in our government agencies, and in our military academies, when we find out that those whom we trusted to live by a higher code of ethics... cheated. Sometimes, it seems as if nearly everyone is trying to shortcut the shortcut!

If we think of the shortcut as the most direct, effective, and efficient route toward the accomplishment of any task or achievement, then it is the ultimate pathway to success for that particular goal. *No matter what the goal, then, the shortcut is the best and most timely way to succeed, and the steps in the path are the principles for succeeding.* These principles are paramount to attaining the goal. Leaving any of them out reduces our chances of success.

It doesn't get any Shorter... than the Shortcut!

In our work, relationships, marriages, lifestyle, personal growth, goals and dreams... there are a set of principles which define the steps down the road to success! Some of the time, you and I intuitively sense the rules and canons we must adhere to if we are to succeed. In our workplace, certain standards govern our performance and determine if we keep our occupation, or lose it. These include basic rules of integrity, such as honesty, morality, going the extra mile, and hard work. A good marriage requires, among other things, a moral commitment, understanding, unselfishness, and self discipline.

Our goals, dreams, and vision also have their own respective principles which will make the difference between achieving, or not achieving.

There is a <u>most efficient way</u> to accomplish something, and there are usually many less efficient paths, most of which will probably never get us there. In the scientific and engineering fields, experts attempt to identify the critical path for any major project. This critical path consists of all those events which <u>must</u> occur, <u>in sequence,</u> if the project is to stay on schedule and on budget. All other non-critical events have some flexibility in when and how they may be accomplished. The critical path represents the shortcut for that particular goal. Any deviation from that path, results in more time, more cost, less efficiency, and, occasionally, failure.

Every worthwhile desire, goal, and dream in your life has its own critical path, or shortcut, a set of guiding principles which will make or break you in reaching that goal. Whether it be your desire for a great marriage, a strong spiritual foundation, development of your mind, or achieving financial freedom... each has its shortcut marking the most effective way, for some perhaps the only way, to get to the top! Failing to adhere to any of the critical principles in the shortcut can only result in coming up short, taking much longer, or failing altogether. *No matter what we're trying to achieve... the path to success doesn't get any shorter, than the shortcut!*

Principles... are Principles!

Principle is defined as "a fundamental truth, a rule of conduct, or a basic part." There are cardinal principles which apply to every aspect of our lives, and govern our success or failure. For our specific dreams and goals, each will have its own unique set of principles which lead specifically to attainment of that particular event or quality.

Basic success principles pertain to everything we do. These are fundamental truths, such as a positive mental attitude, honesty, open-mindedness, applied faith, going the extra mile, and persistence, which impact our success or lack of success in literally any activity we choose.

Specific principles relate to a specific objective. These are part of the critical path for that objective, and violating any of these rules or basics will produce less than desired outcomes. For someone desiring to be a doctor, one principle would be graduating from a qualified medical school. An attorney must similarly complete the requirements for a law degree, and pass the bar exam. A carpenter must grasp the basics of nailing and sawing. The boy scout must meet the qualifications for each badge he receives. For a good marriage, you and I must meet the expectations of our spouse, including loyalty and faithfulness. In your work, you have certain actions and performance standards that you must meet, if you are to be competent, qualified, and employed. We could continue, ad infinitum, but I hope you are understanding that every significant achievement carries its own rules of conduct, principles, which limit our success in that objective.

The Law of the Harvest tells us that we reap what we sow. When we want corn, we must plant corn seeds. If we want a mutually rewarding and satisfying marriage, we must plant and nurture the seeds of a good relationship. A strong spiritual life will only come from planting the seeds that lead to deeper understanding of our spirit and mind. In our livelihoods, we must identify, adopt, and nourish, those seeds (principles) which are critical to creating and maintaining productivity. *It makes no difference why we may not plant the right seeds. If we don't... we will not get the right results! Principles... are principles!*

The High Price... of <u>NOT</u> Paying the Price!

When we do not adhere to the principles, we do not pay the price, and we do not follow the law of sowing and reaping. *Failing to nurture the necessary seeds, can only produce less than the desired results.* Let's think about some of the results, when we don't pay the price for success.

All of us want to love and be loved! Love frequently leads to marriage, and virtually everyone would prefer a happy one. Yet, *through ignorance, lack of commitment, and lack of self-discipline*, many marriages end up "on the rocks." A poor marriage produces frustration, unhappiness, stress and anger. From these emotions come poor decisions and further destructive actions, until nationally we reap the harvest of a 50 percent divorce rate, thousands of broken homes, and hundreds of thousands of children living with only one parent.

No sane person would deny themselves good health. However, sane people everywhere do just that, living on the edge, physically and emotionally, until their health deteriorates beyond the point of no return. *Without commitment to proper diet, exercise, sleep, relaxation, and stress management,* unhealthy lifestyles cost us billions of dollars from strokes, heart attacks, deaths, hypertension, high blood pressure, cancer, obesity, lack of energy, and other stress-related illnesses. Our relationships are substandard, our work productivity is lessened, and our sex lives suffer, when our health is marginal.

Man is a spiritual creature, the only one on this earth capable of rational thought, abstract logic, and a sensitivity to our creation and our future. Most of us want to be fulfilled spiritually. *Lacking the total devotion to develop this part of our nature*, though, we all-too-often drift on the current of reality. Without a sense of our spiritual being, we often suffer from apathy, selfishness, self-centeredness, a sense of emptiness, indifference toward others, and a spiritual void which leaves us wandering aimlessly through life.

Our bodies grow, mature, and change our entire lives. Our minds should grow, as well! Personal growth, both mentally and emotionally, ought to be a goal of every single person. The reality is, sadly, that it is not a priority nor even a goal for most people. *With no plan, program nor desire to improve our minds*, the vast majority of us drift on an endless river of mediocrity. Unwilling to pay the price for developing sound thought habits, we lapse into negative thinking, become closed or narrow minded, fall prey to our perceptions and fears, are victimized by every manner of thought disease we are covering in this book, and come to the end of our lives wishing we had accomplished more than we did. We, our loved ones, our nation, and mankind lose so much, because so many of us never come remotely close to our true potential!

Literally every person wants to have a good lifestyle! Every man and woman would like the time and the resources to be able to live and enjoy life to the fullest. Seeds of success must be sown to reap the rewards of lifestyle, also. *Having no definite major purpose for our lives, as few do, we tend to follow the paths of least resistance, just doing what the great majority does.* As a result, very few of us achieve the hopes and dreams we profess to have. The preponderance of us live average lives, floating along year after year, unable to get ahead yet unwilling to do more. Under the stresses of mediocre lifestyles, our health, marriages, relationships, and futures slowly slip away, until a growing sense of failure overtakes us. In the United States of America, the only things standing between 95 percent of us, and poverty in our later years... are social programs, welfare, or death. Less than one in twenty will ever achieve financial independence, in their lifetimes! Because... *we are unwilling to pay the price for success!*

Why Pay the Price?

Throughout this chapter, we are evaluating another attitude which can hold us back. *Since it is an attitude, this thinking which bargains with the price of success, then we control it and can change it, if we want to.* It is up to each of us, whether to pay the price, or shortcut the shortcut, for our goals and dreams. Why should we at least consider paying the price?

Love and relationships have their cost, but the benefits and rewards are well worth the inconveniences and sacrifices! There is possibly no greater satisfaction on this earth than having a mutual sharing of love, feelings, caring, understanding, unselfishness, and the limitless other qualities of life with another person. *Sowing the seeds of commitment, faithfulness, persistence, time, effort, learning, growing, and so forth, into a relationship can reap a harvest of lifetime happiness.* Ask any couple who have a truly great and loving marriage, and you'll undoubtedly be told that the marriage is one of their greatest treasures!

Likewise, good health doesn't happen by accident! For those who pay the price of daily, lifelong attention to diet, stress, risk factors, and exercise, the benefits are worthwhile. *Better health results in more energy, greater ambition, a more positive attitude, increased focus, a more satisfying sex life, higher productivity, and more.*

Creating a strong spiritual, mental and emotional foundation can only improve our happiness and success potential, it cannot hurt! *Developing these intangibles of our mind can lead to deeper and more caring, unselfish feelings for the world we live in. Greater understanding and knowledge, stronger commitment and persistence, intense motivation and ambition, are among the attributes which lead unerringly to higher levels of success and joy.* These are among the harvest we reap from sowing positive seeds of thought and inspiration into our minds, through an active and lifetime process of conscious personal growth!

A good lifestyle creates a good life! Having the time, income, and resources to pursue the finer things of life, our dreams and goals, are among the higher aspirations, for the typical individual. Lifestyle does not come without a price. For those too-few who will pay the price, though, the riches are numerous! Those who achieve a great lifestyle have the freedom of time and money to do the things they want to do, go to the places they wish to visit, be with the people they care about, and become the kind of men and women they can be genuinely proud of. *Lifestyle is a product of the habits of patience, virtue, integrity, persistence, sincere effort, to name only a few, and may allow us to realize our greatest potential as a human being!*

These are but a few of the more important ideals we may attain, when we're willing to pay the price! There are other, equally worthy aspirations that have their own separate principles and demands. When you and I are willing to do all of what each requires, then we stand the highest chance of reaping the harvest we want.

For those of you who want to learn more about creating success habits, and following those principles which promote achievement, I suggest several excellent resources at the end of this book.

Albert E. N. Gray's words are worth repeating again, from *The Common Denominator of Success* pamphlet: *"The secret of success of every man who has ever been successful... lies in the fact that he formed the habit of doing things that failures don't like to do."*

If we are not willing to do what it takes, we will not get what we might have gotten!

CHAPTER SIXTEEN
PLANNING TO FAIL? OR... FAILING TO PLAN?

Through the decade of the 1960's and into the 70's, the United States was involved in the Vietnam War. The underlying concern was to stop the spread of communism, and the basic fear was that if South Vietnam came under the Red umbrella, other countries of the region would "fall like dominos"! Countless thousands of hours went into planning, preparation, and execution of national, strategic, and tactical battle operations. Yet, with more than 57,000 American soldiers dead, and following years of increasing national debate and opposition to the war effort, in 1975, the US pulled hastily away from South Vietnam, as the communist North poured into the South. Years later, the deep wounds and scars still ooze anger, bitterness, and sadness, across our nation, when the name Vietnam comes up. The Southeast Asia region did not fall like dominos to communism, and, in fact, communism around the world began to crumble and fall, as its internal weaknesses overpowered its external appearance of strength. Despite the planning of thousands of experts, the Vietnam War remains one of America's greatest failures!

During the Frontier Days of the American West, military outposts protected the westward expansion of civilization and commerce across this vast land. At one such outpost, and in one such effort to counter the opposition of the native American Indians, General George Armstrong Custer led a group of soldiers into southern Montana. In the territory known as The Little Bighorns, Custer found out, too late, that he had grossly miscalculated the resolve, skill and numbers of the Native Americans, led by Chiefs Crazy Horse and Sitting Bull. On the grassy hills and valleys of Custer's Last Stand, his army was nearly destroyed, and this event lives in infamy in the annals of American history and folklore.

The Civil War was a dim and bloody chapter in United States history. One footnote from that long war is remembered as "Pickett's Charge"! At Gettysburg, Pennsylvania, in the summer of 1863, Confederate General George Edward Pickett, with 4500 of his foot soldiers, faced the Union battle lines. Despite the cannon barrels they stared into, filled with grape shot, Pickett ordered the charge. In unison, his troops entered into a full run toward the Union guns. With each cannon fired, huge holes were torn in Pickett's line of advancing soldiers. Even the Union men could not believe the damage they were inflicting. By the time Pickett accepted retreat, he had lost over three-fourths of his men.

These examples, and countless others, reveal the absolute devastation that occurs when our planning is weak, inadequate, or not followed. Basing our lives and our activities on bad information, faulty assumptions, and poorly established objectives, we produce some of history's greatest tragedies, when viewed in the national context. *Individually, the stories are seldom disclosed to more than a handful of close observers, but they are no less tragic in their consequences... when we plan to fail, or fail to plan, properly.* In this chapter, we will look into the results we reap when our planning is poor or nonexistent.

Planning to Fail? Nobody Would Do That!

This may seem obvious, on the surface. Very few of us would ever admit that we planned to fail at anything. And yet, why is it that so many people in the United States, and around the world, fail to accomplish anything significant, including most of the dreams and goals they cherished, during their entire lifetimes? Are chance, circumstances, bad luck, and fate... always the culprits? Or, are we perhaps more responsible for our lack of achievement than we'd care to admit? Could we be planning to fail without even realizing it?

Planning is not a hidden art! Most of us could tell someone else how to develop a plan. It's intuitively obvious that we need to first of all establish an **objective or goal** we need or want to satisfy. Then, we must identify the **factors and facts** which will impact the pursuit of our goal, as well as the **key**

assumptions we must logically make in order to have a rational basis for action. We'll need to **identify the alternatives**, our choices of actions that are reasonably available to us; and **determine our strategy and tactics** for dealing with the challenge, as it is limited by our **resources**. The act of planning is actually more of a circle than a straight line, because the objective or goal of our plans is usually affected by a **thoughtful analysis** of the facts, factors, assumptions, alternatives, strategy, tactics, and resources that are realistically available to us. *Limitations in any or all of these areas may require that the objective or goal be adjusted, changed, postponed, or given up altogether.* Ultimately, our planning should yield a **best course of action** by which we may pursue our objective. Then, of course, we will need a process of continual **follow-up** to adjust our plans as other elements change unexpectedly.

Think back to those times you were in school, or taking a course of instruction. When it came time to take a test, we had to plan and prepare for that test, if we were to make a satisfactory grade. Shortcomings in any of our planning areas, could affect the outcome. If we set our objective as just passing, with no intention of doing our best, this would effect how we prepared. Compare that to the goal of getting the highest grade in the class. One factor which always applied is "what chapters or sections or concepts do I study and focus on"? Our evaluation of this factor determined what and how we studied. Alternatives could range from not studying at all, to cramming the night before, to days of in-depth review, to hiring a tutor. Our goal would partially dictate which alternative we chose; and the limitations of time and other resources would possibly make us change our goal, and the preparation alternative we could reasonably select. Assumptions, such as how difficult it was going to be, how everyone else would do, and whether or not a grading curve would apply, could impact our choices and decision.

This simple example demonstrates the planning that we do, everyday, usually without putting it into a formal planning process. Now, what happens if we arbitrarily make faulty assumptions? Such as assuming that everyone will do poorly, and there will be a grading curve. Or, we assume the test will be so easy that we don't need to study for it? Dare we make that assumption? Maybe, we decide the test will cover only a few common concepts, rather than being comprehensive. This would effect how we study and prepare. And, what if we had no goal at all? We would just study until it felt like we'd studied enough, if we studied at all. This would certainly govern how well we do! *When we approach any challenge, including our life, with unrealistic assumptions, poor factors or information, no analysis of logical alternatives, and, quite often, without clear objectives or goals... this is the same as planning to fail!*

We might as well plan to fail, when we don't make a logical, thoughtful analysis of the facts, factors, meaningful assumptions, resource limitations, and sensible alternatives, which lead toward goals or objectives. Sometimes, this breakdown occurs out of sheer laziness, we just don't want to take the time and effort to be thorough. Other times, preconceived ideas and conclusions may convince us that we have the solution already, so we don't think through or plan out a major decision. We believe what we want to believe, and don't gamble that facts may prove us wrong. *Whatever the motive, when we only pay lip service to planning, and don't elect to do it properly or thoroughly, the results will most often be less than we wanted.*

"Poor Planning" Equals "Failing to Plan"!

General George Armstrong Custer had several options available to him prior to attacking the Native American Indians at Little Big Horn. However, based on poor information (not knowing that he was attacking such a large encampment), and apparently assuming it was a "normal" sized party, which would probably try to flee under attack, Custer chose to attack without waiting for nearby reinforcements. *Plans, based upon bad information, usually lead to disastrous results!*

Several years ago, while I was still on active duty in the military, I happened to read an article concerning a study of post-military retirement. Among other things, the study revealed that the average military retiree lived less than 18 months after retiring. I was profoundly affected by this information! How could that be, for it meant that most of us were dying before the age of 65? Could it be that we are *assuming* too much for retirement, and thereby not making adequate plans for our years following military life? I believe that this does, indeed, play a major part in the stresses, strains, poor health, and premature death that frequently accompanies a major change of lifestyle. We assume we'll "have it made," and, therefore, we do little to prepare!

Making plans is a fact of life! Whether you or I use a formal planning process, or just "wing it," we go through life making plans of one sort or another. Seldom do we stop to consider that the elements which affect any planning process, formal or informal, are elements which directly impact the success or failure of any plans. *Poor or faulty information* will virtually always lead to poor plans and undesired outcomes! Even knowing this fact, many times we base major decisions on poor information, and then complain about our "bad luck" when we don't succeed. Far too often, when you and I want validation and guidance, especially concerning money or occupation matters, we turn to those who know little more than we know. Rather than seek the advice of real experts, who have done what we'd like to do, we ask a relative or a best friend. Even worse, we often follow their advice, and it's frequently not worth much!

Often our *assumptions* are faulty, yet we base our major life decisions upon them! An example could be an assumption that we'll be able to live with financial freedom and dignity, on the 40 percent retirement pension we expect to receive. Other times, we fail to take stock of our available *resources*, which can realistically be put toward our plans and goals. This can result in both under or over-estimating our future capabilities. If I downplay my ability to change and adapt to new situations,

I may limit my choices of alternatives to only those which I am currently familiar with, and eliminate those thousands of options I might have had. When I don't identify and consider all reasonable *alternatives*, I limit my potential for succeeding. Worst of all, *if I do not clearly determine my definite major purpose, and my dreams, wants, and needs, my plans lack* **the most important element of all... an objective!**

Poor planning, based upon faulty or omitted information and elements, usually has the same result as if we didn't plan at all! We fail to accomplish our goal! Maybe we make some progress, but coming up short still isn't the same as getting it done. Especially when our failure is the result of inadequate, improper, lackadaisical or non-existent planning, it is particularly inexcusable! Would it have mattered at Little Big Horn, if Custer had just not planned at all, but raced helter-skelter into battle without a second thought? Does it matter that our Vietnam War experiences resulted, in part, from improper assumptions and poor use of resources? We still lost 50,000 American lives, billions of dollars, and the war. Do you and I care why we find ourselves unable to live the retired lifestyle we wanted? By then, is it important to know that we spent years relying upon bad assumptions? *No matter the reasons, the results we reap from poor and flawed planning... are usually as unfavorable as if we had not planned at all!*

The Result is the Same.... Failure!

History is full of evidence that bad plans, or no plans, usually end up in the same place... failing to meet objectives! Virtually every war ever fought had victors and losers directly related to the effectiveness of their planning. On an individual basis, the winners and losers in the game of life can generally attribute their status to the strength or weakness in their life's plans. *It makes little difference what the goals are, if our plans do not include realistic and accurate assumptions, factual and worthwhile information, an intelligent assessment of our resources, identification of all logical alternatives, a sound strategy for progressing, and a clear picture of what we hope*

*or need to accomplish... they are very apt to produce
unsatisfactory results!*

If the results are truly what we want, desire, or need to
achieve, then the inability to achieve them, for whatever reason,
constitutes failure. It does not matter whether that condition is
the result of poor planning, no planning, or planning to fail...
we still didn't succeed!

Trusting Our Most Cherished Goals... to Luck!

I've heard it said that most people devote more time and
thought to planning a two-week vacation, than they do to
planning their life's work! Sadly, both my experience and
observation would indicate that this is true. We will plan
carefully for frivolous events, while at the same time: *we trust
our most important dreams and goals... to pure luck, chance
and circumstance!*

Few of us even know what we want out of life! Without a
dream, goal, vision or objective, it is literally impossible to
formulate meaningful plans and produce effective efforts. Yet,
this is where the vast majority of us are. Napoleon Hill said
that "...98 out of every one-hundred people..." have no
"...definite major purpose..." in their lives. They just wander
through life "... like a ship without a rudder...""! Knowing what
we want to accomplish, is a critical part of any planning
process. Our life is our most important operation! Whether we
admit it or not, we are in a constant process of planning and
living our lives. ***Lacking a definite major purpose or an
objective***, *virtually guarantees that we will be inconsistent and
ineffective in all the remaining plans and outcomes.*

Many of us base our key decisions upon faulty assumptions!
Where our life plans are concerned, some of these assumptions
may be things like: "just get a good education, and a good job,
and it will work out!"; "a good job, with good benefits, is all I
need!"; "hard work is all it takes!"; "keep your nose clean, and
you'll get by!"; "don't rock the boat, and you'll make it to

retirement!"; and "all I need to do is stick it out until retirement, and then I'll live like I want!" *We often fail because we fail to investigate the facts!* We assume what we should not assume. Take just one myth: "hard work is all it takes." If this were true, then nearly all housewives, ranchers, farmers, waiters, waitresses, busboys, carpenters, steamfitters, and ditchdiggers... should be wealthy. They aren't! Take another myth: "a retirement pension represents a good lifestyle." The federal government statistics disprove this, for they show that about 95% of us will require federal, state, or family assistance, or continued employment... just to live in our later years. *Poor assumptions lead invariably to poor results, especially where our lives are concerned!*

We often sacrifice our planning potential for a herd mentality. *With a herd mentality, we follow the herd instead of thinking and planning for ourselves!* We make the assumption that the majority, or herd, has the answer, and we do what they do. Rather than even consider being in business for ourselves, 95% of us work as employees for someone else. Most people make no effort to improve their minds nor their decision-making skills, and we follow their example. The great majority will take, and follow, advice... only from the great majority. Therefore, the great majority's opinions are seldom challenged and few people change their circumstances nor their lives, for the better. They just follow the taillights to work, and back home again in the evening. And, when they have to stop working, the great majority wonders what went wrong that they can't live as they thought they could live!

All too often, we trust our most treasured dreams, to vehicles incapable of delivering them! Instead of basing our financial choices upon what dreams we hope to achieve, we instead follow the herd and take the easy path of least resistance. *This amounts to making plans and decisions without considering all reasonable alternatives!* This is what we do if we only consider employment as our major financial option. The same if we only consider taking over the family business, because of the tradition we must uphold. If our military leaders made war plans in this manner, we would scream for their heads! Yet, you and I think nothing of basing our lifetime occupation and dreams... on only the easy and familiar choices!

The result, of failing to adequately plan within the context of our lives, is that few of us achieve what we want. In one of the Earth's most prosperous nations, the vast majority of people live in mediocrity, compared to their potential! Divorce claims most marriages, and too many of our children seek comfort outside of society's boundaries. We suffer from decimated spirits, which shows up in unhappiness, depression, and stress-related illnesses. Nobody could even guess how much potential good is lost... because we fail to properly plan our dreams and our lives!

Where the Rubber Meets the Road!

The Vietnam War was a huge tragedy for the United States, as much because *plans weren't followed*, as because planning was faulty! Despite the involvement of thousands of military experts, plans were often ignored by political decision-makers. President Johnson reportedly retained even the most basic military targeting and strategy decisions at his level, thereby thwarting the inputs of his best military minds in the process. Decisions were perhaps too concerned with the political ramifications, rather than with the successful prosecution of the war effort. In the final analysis, this war seemed to be fought *without a goal* of winning it. Thousands of lives were wasted, in part because of *flawed assumptions* which led to our involvement, and partly because our *actions were not consistent with our stated plans* and intentions.

As with the war in Vietnam, *plans are worthless unless followed through with coherent and consistent action!* In the Air Force, we said this was "where the rubber meets the road." My grandmother used to say the "proof was in the pudding." Planning, by itself, will never get us the outcomes we desire. Only when we take the efforts of our planning; and apply skill, work, and persistence; combined with a willingness to evaluate, update, and change our plans as factors change, will we have a possibility of seeing the results we want. In other words... *no matter how good our plans are, it still takes appropriate action and persistent, determined effort to get it done!*

Plan to Succeed!

Few plans will be of much value, unless the **goals and objectives** are clearly thought out and written out. *This one step is often the most neglected, especially where our lives are concerned, and almost guarantees faulty plans and undesirable results.* A definite major purpose for our lives is likened to having a grand national objective behind military war plans. Without this overall guiding light, an all-encompassing goal, none of our secondary plans may have the proper direction and objectives. If you have not clearly identified your definite major purpose for living and working and loving... it would be very worthwhile for you to do so!

Realize that our decisions are usually based upon one or more **assumptions**. Therefore, the quality of our decisions, and the results we get from them, will relate directly to the accuracy of the assumptions we've used! Many of us use the assumptions of the "herd," the great majority, without attempting to clearly and logically think through our own. For this reason, we end up making the kind of assumptions we noted earlier, another example being: "do what most people are doing, and you'll make it." Make it where? The reality is that if we only do what the herd is doing, we'll probably get what the herd has got... mediocrity, at best. *Give as much careful analysis and thought and investigation to your assumptions, as to any part of your planning... they are critical to your outcome!*

*Where important decisions are concerned, seldom are we going to have all the **facts and factors** accurately identified, without doing some **investigation and homework**.* Our decisions are influenced by the facts that we base them on. It follows, then, that the outcomes will also be affected by our facts, or lack of facts, used in making our plans and decisions. This seems obvious, and yet very few of us actually researched the work or occupation that we have! The last time you had a chance to look at a business, job, or investment opportunity, did you really make a thorough and logical investigation and analysis of the facts... before making a decision? Or, did you do what most people do, and base your decision on perceptions (perhaps misperceptions?), assumptions (maybe faulty?), preconceived ideas (possibly wrong ones?), and opinions (what if they are inaccurate?)? There is a computer term called GIGO. This means that if you put "garbage in," you'll get "garbage out" of your computer. Where our lives are concerned, this is also applicable. *If we base our most important life-affecting decisions on garbage information, we'll undoubtedly reap garbage rewards!*

Ask any person if they'd like to have choices in life, and you'll hear an almost unanimous "yes." We envy people who have options. At the same time, though, you and I often ignore or eliminate the choices we do have, when it comes to planning our lives! Many of us put on the blinders when deciding what to do for a living and how to live our lives. Rather than truly evaluate ***all reasonable options***, we usually have a preconceived path we intend to follow, and we exclude all others. *Planning becomes nearly worthless, when we only allow ourselves to have one alternative!*

In some plans, we may want to identify a ***strategy*** for pursuing our objective. An example might be found in an objective of becoming financially independent. We could seek this objective in many ways: through employment; having a business; investing; or a combination of these. A strategy of using any and all legal means in combination, will differ from a strategy of using employment only.

Recognize that a key resource at our disposal is the advice and counsel of others. *Recognize also that **advice and counsel** is only beneficial when it comes from someone who knows what they're talking about!* Most of us only seek the advice of family or friends, those who sometimes have even less credibility than we do, in the areas we are considering. However, there are many very successful people who are more than willing to take the time to advise us, if we only ask. Others have written excellent books, or even made video or audio tapes, which can help steer us in the right directions. One such author is Napoleon Hill, in particular his discussions regarding "definite major purpose" and "mastermind." It is a very wise business decision to use the experience of others to help us make good decisions, and to avoid the pitfalls.

The underlying objective of any planning is to **determine the best alternative**, or alternatives, from among our choices available. Our success or failure depends on all the inputs used in the evaluation... our facts, factors, assumptions, advice, strategy, alternatives, and goals. Inadequate thought, investigation, and analysis of any element, will degrade the ultimate choice we make and reduce our effectiveness in reaching our goal. Likewise, *we may have all the elements, perfectly, but if we don't do a thoughtful and logical analysis, our results will still suffer.*

Ultimately, the "rubber meets the road" as we place **action, work, commitment, consistency, and persistency into the alternative(s)** we've chosen. Only this, and the willingness to make the followup adjustments as circumstances change and more facts become available, will produce the positive results we desire.

Where our lives are concerned, it makes little difference if we plan to fail, fail to plan, plan improperly, or don't follow-up on our plans... the result will still be mediocrity!

CHAPTER SEVENTEEN
ARE YOU BRAIN-DEAD?

He was a good young man, with a family and a reasonably good job. But, he seemed to have so much more promise than what he was showing! Mark appeared to lack confidence in himself, and was your typical wall flower, anytime he was around people he was unfamiliar with. Outside of his work and family, his passions were watching television, video movies, and playing computer games and video arcades. He also loved to play most sports, especially basketball, and seldom missed a chance to play. His father cared about him deeply, but sometimes became very frustrated with Mark because of his seemingly wasted potential, doing what he was doing. Mark just didn't seem interested in reaching for all that life offered!

The old cowboys relaxed in the pickup, watching the rancher struggle with the heavy pails of milk as he walked from the barn where he'd just milked their five cows. A scruffy mutt barked at his heels, chickens flew in all directions, four kids were in hot pursuit, and a hog rooted near the gate of their dilapidated yard fence and shanty. His weathered face showed the concerns of a difficult life. The one cowboy asked the other: "I hear the boss wanted to go to that college in town and get an ejication, but decided he couldn't. Why was that?" The other answered: "He figgered if he got that ejication, he might ferget how good he has it here!"

Do you know anyone like these folks? If so, can you review the past year, five years, or even ten years of their lives and see any significant changes? For that matter, *can you look back over your own life for the past five or ten years, and identify any serious changes for the better in yourself? Are you a much better man or woman today... than you were ten years ago?* Are you more ambitious, driven, determined, persistent, focused, knowledgeable, now than when you first entered the workforce? If your honest appraisal is that you have not grown as much as you wished, perhaps this chapter is for you. In the following sections, we'll help you see if you're ***mentally*** *stagnating*, going nowhere with your personal development and growth, and what you can do if you wish to change this direction.

Symptoms of a Stagnant Mind!

A stagnant mind has many symptoms! We'll try to point out a few candidates that might relate to you, or to someone you know. Let's use the old wisdom: If you want to know the tree... check the fruit!. So, the first "fruit" that we'll look at is how we spend the precious hours of our days, years, and life.

The way you and I spend our leisure and discretionary time will tell us a great deal about our personal and mental growth! The first fruit may be one of the most revealing. How much time do we spend watching television? Surveys show that the average American spends as much time watching television as is spent making a living. If we are even close to average, have you thought about how this impacts our life? An average television viewer just sits in front of their set with their brain in neutral, watching screen characters live life. What could you accomplish if you used that time to develop your mind?

Similarly, are you a person who devotes considerable time to watching videos, playing computer games, at the arcade, and other related activities? What more could you achieve, if you used that time for self-improvement? In the same way, many of us have the habit of reading novels, tabloid journals, and other types of fiction. While we all need some time for the pure pursuit of enjoyment, we can spend a disproportionate amount of our time in these activities? Many of us are sports fanatics, and we spend much of our free time either watching or playing various sports. One who isn't growing mentally probably spends far more time, on activities like sports, than a recreational interest should warrant? Can we afford to let that time get away?

Another symptom of mental stagnation is the way we relate to other people. The man or woman who isn't growing mentally and emotionally has a tendency to avoid people situations they find uncomfortable. We are probably uneasy interacting with strangers at public gatherings, parties, and other social events. We might shun discussions outside our areas of interest. Dodging new people and discourse which challenge our thinking are likely signs of a person who isn't growing mentally.

How do you view the overall fruit of your life? Do you feel like you're in a rut, with little changing? Are you essentially the same man or woman you were ten years ago? Have you accepted that life's as good now as it will ever be? If these questions make you uncomfortable, and your answers would be more "yes" than "no," *you probably have a lot of potential that you're not using!*

Consider this thought: *"We don't know what we're missing"!* Few expressions are truer, in the area of personal growth. Most people have literally no idea how much more they could be and do, if they just challenged themselves more. Few of us have tried to evaluate our full potential. Likewise, most are not familiar with the resources available to stimulate personal growth and achievement. *Totally blind to our own vast capabilities, we settle for mundane and mediocre existences, without ever cracking open the door to glimpse the great things we were capable of doing and becoming.*

When We Don't Know... What We Don't Know (about ourselves)!

The great majority of us have no idea how much we don't know about our own potential! As a result of this ignorance, we acquire many undesirable traits and qualities, and we seem unable to control our own lives.

An individual who exhibits signs of mental laziness lives a generally mundane and mediocre life. They tend to focus on doing those things they are familiar with, and they rarely challenge themselves on anything new or different. They show little interest in knowledge beyond their own specific areas of concern. As a result, this person can become very one-dimensional, and may be very boring to other people. This tends to trap them where they are, because they seldom come out of their mental shell.

Mental laziness leads to attitude habits, such as closed-mindedness, unaccountability, and making excuses, which add bars to our mind's prison of mediocrity. Our unwillingness to relate to new people keeps us out of intelligent and stimulating conversations. Lacking interaction with other people and ideas, we may create faulty people, reasoning, and logic skills, which lead inevitably to poor decisions. Over our lifetimes, these habits produce an inability to progress as we desired, and often leave us without purpose, feeling worthless and unmotivated.

Without motivation, a mind is like an arm whose nerves have been damaged. With no guiding impulses to activate the muscles in the arm, it hangs limp and useless. An unmotivated mind also hangs in a limp and useless state! A person who lacks mental growth and stimulation, also lacks vision, dreams, and goals. Without this sense of purpose and excitement for their future... there is no motivation.

When we don't recognize our own potential, we just drift through life... uninspired! Without inspiration, our lives are dull, unemotional, uneventful. Inspiration comes most frequently from the lives and stories of other people. The mind that is disinterested in people and growth, will probably be very uninspired.

In our modern world, as new technologies are developed, and as our society becomes increasingly global, you and I must be in a constant state of growth... if we are just to keep up. If we aren't growing, mentally and emotionally, then we are actually falling behind! And... *just because we aren't aware of our lost potential... doesn't mean we aren't still losing it!*

151

Nobody can talk as interestingly as the feller that's not hampered by facts or information. (Kin Hubbard)

As One of the Living...!

The most successful, happy, and well-rounded people I know, have a **hunger for knowledge** and a habit of stimulating their brains through the thoughts of other people. This can be done in several ways, from formal schooling to a self-study reading program, from adult education classes to invigorating conversations with people who excel in life. All of us know that when we exercise, we build stronger muscle fibers, increase strength and endurance, and create both a physical and emotional tone which gives us an edge in other areas of our lives. The same is true of exercising and strengthening our minds. Whatever means we use to expand our minds, the fruits are almost certain to be sweet!

Every human being needs something in their life which gives them a reason for being, for doing, for becoming. **Motivation** is a crucial reason to join the living, and *the person who knows what he or she wants out of life, who has dreams and goals, a vision for their life, is a person who has activated their brain with hope and belief in the future!*

Inspiration is a multiplying factor to motivation! Just as the cry of a child adds tenderness and love to our embrace, so does inspiration enhance our desire to achieve our fondest dreams. Those who are history's achievers, are usually those who are inspired leaders and do-ers. Inspiration is a by-product of studying and learning from the experiences, failures, and successes of others. The stimulating and inspiring thoughts and examples of our fellow man serve to propel us forward in our own lives.

Personal growth produces better powers of reasoning and logic and more fruitful decisions. It helps us identify and reduce bad habits, while finding and promoting those useful ones which improve our success potential. Individual mental growth yields a harvest of such qualities as integrity, honesty, accountability, persistence, caring, and ultimately... character!

   Just as our bodies need exercise if they are to remain in peak condition and health, so do our minds need **stimulation** if they are to serve us well for a lifetime! My hometown newspaper (Hyannis, Nebraska, the *Grant County News*) reported that a recent study by several universities indicates that people may be able to control the death of their brain cells by using their brain power throughout life. Researchers found that those who aged the most gracefully and had the least mental decline were those who had the most years of schooling. We can read between the lines of such information, and it is easy to conclude that formal schooling isn't the key... *stimulating and challenging the brain on a consistent basis, is the key!* This article concluded with the following: "The Nebraska Medical Association recommends that you exercise not only your body, but your brain, as well, by reading and engaging in thought-provoking recreation."

How to Come Alive!

   While nobody knows for certain what our mental capacity is, present research indicates that most of us use less than 10% of our brain's capabilities! Can you imagine what could be accomplished if we doubled or tripled that? Here are some suggestions which can help those of you who are interested in the challenge of becoming the *best you*.

   The key to maintaining peak mental performance seems to be *stimulating, exercising, and challenging our brain*. Formal schooling is a start and gives most of us our boost into the adult world, but this usually becomes less of a factor as we mature. The majority of us will enter the "school of hard knocks," following our formal education, and this is where we find our greatest opportunities for self-growth. There are some of our best teachers: trial and error, pain, disappointment, failure, success, experience, and time, to name a few. However, we can avoid much of the time and disappointments if we use the experiences, knowledge, mistakes, successes, and wisdom of those who have gone before us. Using the books, video and audio tapes, advice, counsel, guidance, and mentorship of those who know what we don't know, you and I can learn what they know without making their mistakes.

Self-study *holds the greatest promise of personal development, for most of us!* Self-study is affordable to even the pauper, in our libraries, and is obtainable within the time limitations of the busiest person. It may be substituted for those activities of lesser importance, and fit in among our priorities. A common thread among highly successful men and women is that they take charge of their personal development with an on-going program for *self-improvement*. Benjamin Franklin is one example of a great thinker and leader who kept himself in a lifetime program of character development and personal growth. You and I can do the same!

Keep in mind that it's never too late to become a better "you"! Our bodies reach their physical peak in our teens or twenties, but evidence suggests that our brains don't reach their peak until much later. Regardless of your age, you can improve your chances for aging with greater dignity and grace, by stimulating and challenging your brain on a continual basis!

A well known slogan says "A mind is a terrible thing to waste". *Your mind... and your life... are too important to waste.*

"There is no education like adversity."
(Benjamin Disraeli)

"The art of living lies less in eliminating our troubles than in growing with them." (Bernard M. Baruch)

CHAPTER EIGHTEEN
SHACKLED.... IN A POOR RELATIONSHIP?

Jim and Betty had been married for nine years, and had two children. The first few years, they had a loving relationship. However, the last four years had brought increasing stress from Jim's work, which demanded long hours and an indefinite schedule. The children's activities kept Betty on the go constantly, as well, and she seemed to have little time for her husband. They were drifting apart, and neither knew what to do about it. While they both had big dreams, they couldn't agree on how to change for the better. Everything they might have tried to improve their outlook, was always dashed by arguments and disagreement. The years drifted by, and Jim and Betty found themselves increasingly frustrated, discontent, and unhappy.

Dick and Jane never imagined they'd be in this situation! Their marriage of twenty years was over, and they and their four offspring were trying to make the difficult adjustments that go with splitting years of memories in half. When they married, they were so much in love they couldn't believe anything would ever come between them. But, as they charged into the corporate world, going separate directions in their professions, the stress and challenges of life in the fast lane began to take their toll. By the tenth year, they had difficulty communicating, and their only common ground was the children. Dick became totally immersed in his work. Jane focused so much on her work and the children that she would forget she was even married. When the first child left for college, Jane realized that life was passing her by and she was not happy. She filed for divorce, and nothing Dick could say or do would change her mind. After a messy and costly court battle, the remaining assets were divided and, broken and broke, they started over.

These tragic tales, sadly, represent over 50 percent of all US marriages! Fractured relationships leave most of our marriages and families in pain and bitterness. Not only that, but *poor relationships, especially in marriage, are perhaps one of the greatest reasons behind a national plague of cynicism, unhappiness, hopelessness, and failure. Taken in total, these seeds of discontent bring forth a mighty harvest of lost potential... and mediocrity!* Together, we'll try to look at why a "bad marriage (relationship)" holds us back and what we might do to improve it.

What I Am... and Am Not!

Up front, I want you to understand where I am coming from in this chapter. I am simply a middle-aged, college educated, former professional, now businessman and writer, who has been around a while and is a good observer of people. Besides that, I have been educated in the "School of Hard Knocks," having went through one divorce and experiencing similar challenges in other relationships before finally realizing I needed to do something different. The "something different" was to seek knowledge about relationships by reading, listening, and learning from those who know more than I do about such things. In this chapter, I am drawing upon five years of study, and a lifetime of observations and personal experiences, to share with you, the reader, wisdom and suggestions that I believe can be worthwhile and constructive.

I am NOT a trained marriage counselor, nor a psychologist or psychiatrist! I don't have any degree or formal education in the field of human behavior or relationships. While I am capable of sharing worthwhile experiences and beliefs about the institution of marriage with you, I do not want to give the impression that I have all the answers for any one of you. *My goal is to give you a different perspective about marriage than maybe you've had before, and to stimulate you to take whatever additional steps you may believe appropriate in the pursuit of a more satisfying relationship with the person you've chosen to go through life with.*

When It's Wrong... It Stinks!

Nearly all long-term relationships, especially marriages, begin with strong positive feelings, such as those of love, devotion, caring, and commitment. However, when the situations, challenges, and circumstances of life have chipped away at our original values and feelings, over time, we can lose our positive emotions to the onslaught of negative ones. In my experiences, these unwanted changes may be slow, subtle, and almost imperceptible to the people affected by them. We don't usually recognize that they're happening until a particular crisis or event causes us to look back... and look hard at where we are! By the time we acknowledge that we aren't satisfied, unwanted changes have already gained a foothold. As a marriage deteriorates, so too do those qualities and values we hold dear.

As a man and woman find it more and more difficult to relate effectively with one another, a *sense of discontentment* begins to grow. Over time, occasional disagreements and arguments can intensify into frequent verbal (or physical) fighting, abuse, and an overriding sense of anger. Criticism often evolves into a daily and persistent habit of fault-finding and condemnation of our partner. As the relationship goes from bad to worse, the frustration and complaints become constant companions. The dissatisfaction slowly gives way to a feeling of unhappiness.

A bad relationship creates a persistent atmosphere of unhappiness, frustration, and hopelessness. *It can become our dominating thought*, and begin to crowd out our other priorities. Time and energy that should be spent on children, work, personal health, and similarly important subjects, are frequently allocated to worry, anger, bitterness, and doubt. Preoccupation with a poor marriage can effectively destroy our ambition and motivation to go forward in life, both in our work and personal lives. The person who previously excelled, may fall into a melancholy state of just getting by, while their mind plays the tapes of discontent over and over.

It has been my experience and observation, that as men plunge deeper into frustration and despair from a poor marriage, we tend to *withdraw from our spouse*. A husband may even ignore the nagging and criticisms which used to elicit his angry response. His only exceptions may be the occasional "blow-up" when he cannot ignore his spouse's particularly stinging comments. He also will immerse himself in his job, a hobby, sports, or another activity, as a way to divert his attention from an unhappy relationship at home. Should our frustrations become great enough, we may eventually seek other relationships which are prone to be destructive. These relationships may be "with the guys," at the local after-work places, or even with another woman.

Women, on the other hand, tend to handle marital frustration and unhappiness in slightly different ways. Initially, in my perception, a woman is likely to *voice her frustrations* to her husband. When that is ineffective, she may become more vocal and critical of her man, finding fault with him at every opportunity, and can engage in persistent nagging. She may eventually *withdraw from him*, and their communication may almost entirely cease. As their ability to relate verbally declines, so does their sexual relationship become less fulfilling. Often, she will substitute a close friend, male or female, as her confidant, shutting out her husband even more. When the frustrations reach an intolerable level, she may take the drastic step of separating herself from him, perhaps moving out altogether or developing a relationship with another man. In the advanced stages, despair and hopelessness can result in separation, infidelity, and ultimately divorce.

In the final analysis, a bad marriage relationship retards our ability to progress in life! It can so completely consume our energy, time, and thoughts that we have little remaining to put toward more constructive goals. Unable to focus our abilities on moving forward, we become trapped between the "blame game" of the past and the sad plight of the present. As our union disintegrates, it not only wastes our current resources but limits our future potential, as well. ***Filled with the negative*** *emotions of doubt, fear, anger, worry, unhappiness, and despair, we are placed squarely on the path leading toward failure!* Why is it that the most important relationship we have, that between husband and wife, can often go so painfully wrong?

We Don't Know... What We Don't Know!

I can relate from personal experience, observation, and self-study that very few of us, men or women, have a base of practical knowledge for building strong and lasting relationships. From the very beginning, we operate in the realm of ignorance and inaccurate thinking about how to foster a lifelong and mutually satisfying relationship with our mate.

Men and women are different, and we do indeed think differently! This is "common knowledge" that we joke about, but seldom understand. All of us recognize the physical differences which intrigue and attract us. Few of us, though, understand that our cellular and organic structures are significantly distinct between male and female, and that our brains operate differently. Experts tell us that men tend to think logically, while women think emotionally. Males are usually very focused, "one-track-minded," and visually stimulated; while the average female can concentrate on a wide array of details at once, and is stimulated more by words than by sight. A man is naturally oriented to the future, while our ladies are inclined toward the present. A man becomes sexually aroused quickly by sight, while the typical woman must warm to the passion over time by words and feelings. This list of differences could continue, but you are probably sensing by now that our spouses <u>are</u> uniquely different from us!

If men and women are truly quite unlike, and our scientific understanding is still evolving, is it surprising that prior generations, including many of our parents, have gone through life in total ignorance of such unique qualities? If our grandfathers and grandmothers did not know and teach our parents how to understand and work successfully with our different traits, how could our parents teach us? If you and I don't learn these things, how can we pass on the knowledge to our own children? And, they to our grandchildren? *We don't know... what we don't know!*

There is a school of thought that believes opposites attract! Many counselors base their techniques on this theory, and much evidence supports it. They believe we are naturally drawn to personality traits opposite to our own. A shy person is attracted to an outgoing one. The talkative personality likes the quiet listener. One who is thoughtful and analytical will feel renewed by the fun and spontaneous type. He is very positive, yet attracted to a skeptical woman. If this theory is accurate, and it seems to be, then the potential gap between husbands and wives widens even further, and communications and understanding become even greater challenges.

Our media-orientation is also a source of confusion and misinformation concerning the way men and women relate to each other. Television is a dominating factor in most households, and the portrayals of the sexes are frequently outlandish and immoral. Our prime-time "education" teaches that dishonesty, deceit, unhappiness, infidelity, and divorce are almost inevitable. Other forms of entertainment send the same messages, and we absorb them. For many of us, we replay the scripts of Hollywood... in our personal lives and relationships!

Few of us go into marriage without some form of personal baggage from our past! Some of us grew up in verbally or physically abusive homes, and too many have even been sexually abused. Others frequently have lived with dysfunctional families, where our role models may have been unable to effectively communicate with or lead the family. Over half of us have personally witnessed and felt the impact of separation, abandonment, infidelity, and divorce. Most of us, who bring such pain into our marriages, will have a difficult time separating the past from the present and future.

Many marriages start off with one foot on a bar of soap! A great many of us rush into this relationship with very little preparation, far too quickly, and sometimes for the wrong reasons. We often have only a superficial knowledge of the man or woman we're marrying, and how to relate to them. Some of us compound this problem by marrying at a very young age, before we've experienced an independent adult life. Sooner or later, this lack of "self" may lead to dissatisfaction with the obligations of marriage. Add children to this mixture, in the first months and years of the relationship, and we set ourselves up to fail because we have little opportunity to develop our understanding and communication skills with each other and to grow together.

With so many misunderstood differences and barriers between us and our mates, is it any wonder that we are unable to understand and communicate? Is it surprising that more than half of all our marriages end in failure? These problems are passed on from generation to generation because few of our ancestors understood them any better than we have. Schools devote little time or resources to studying these challenges, so there is limited opportunity to develop relationship skills in a formal education. Our primary education comes from trial and error, for most of us. A fortunate few may obtain marriage or other counseling. A few of us will teach ourselves by studying the books and other resources that experts make available to us. *However, for the vast majority, husbands and wives continue to not know... what they don't know!*

Grow Together... Or, Grow Apart!

It's challenging enough just to deal with the differences between ourselves and our spouses, and to try and understand the barriers imposed by our past experiences, but we also have to adapt to change! And, in the complex world of the twentieth and twenty-first centuries, change has never been more inevitable nor fast-paced. *Change demands that even in the best relationships and marriages, a man and woman must either grow together... or, they will grow apart!*

Change is one of life's constants! Every species, and every individual creature, is in a persistent process of changing and adapting, aging and dying. The unliving elements, and our earth itself, are in a constant state of growth or deterioration, expansion or contraction. Human societies also change, evolve, and adapt as new ideas, knowledge, inventions, and opportunities surface. During the past one-hundred years, our travel went from horsedrawn buggies to space shuttles. The economic system within the United States has evolved from small rural farms to big urban industries. Where families used to live comfortably on one income of the primary breadwinner, today both spouses usually work separate jobs to finance their lifestyle. Every aspect of our lives is in constant change and these changes inevitably affect how we relate to our spouses and children.

Some changes are helpful, and some are not. All changes, good and bad, which we are not adequately prepared for, cause stresses and strains within our marriages. Stress, itself, is a factor in our health and emotional well-being. Should we not deal effectively with either the changes or the stresses from them, our physical, mental, and emotional makeup can deteriorate. As we suffer individually, our attitudes and reactions can cause negative shockwaves within our most precious relationships. *Under the pressure of changes, stresses, and strains, even once strong marriages can begin to crack!*

Since no relationship is ever perfect, we all have personality differences and past baggage, and with the unwavering onslaught of change; marriages require flexibility, creativity, knowledge... and the willingness to grow! To adapt a relationship based on love, into a marriage based on communication, understanding, and growth... as well as love... demands that the couple change and grow, together. We must become lifelong students of our mate, and be willing to recognize and make changes in ourselves which enhance our marriage. *If either spouse fails to do this, they literally guarantee that the other person will grow away from them, and their marriage will ultimately suffer.* **We will either grow** *together... or, we __will__ grow apart!*

One man's failure is another man's wife.

"I Do?"... Or, "Maybe I Do?"

A major factor which leads to unhappiness, divorce, and most other crises within our marriages, is our own lack of commitment! We all know that commitment means "a promise or a pledge," and that our vows of marriage are a promise, pledge, and commitment to our spouse. However, this knowledge seems to be very short-lived. For many of us, our commitment is conditional upon everything being as we thought it would be.

Nearly every marriage vow contains words to the effect of "for better or for worse, in sickness and in health, till death do us part." There is perhaps no greater commitment, promise, or pledge that we will ever make to another person. In effect, we are giving our word of honor that we will remain loyal and devoted to our partner, no matter what comes our way, and for our lifetime. It comes down to this: *do we mean what we promise, or do we not?*

Granted, there are some circumstances when divorce may be a justified alternative. But, this is certainly not the case in over 50 percent of all marriages! The *"irreconcilable differences" which end most marriages are often just an unwillingness to learn how to relate to, communicate with, understand, and love our spouse.* Yet, are not these challenges just a part of "for better or worse"? Are our problems unchangeable absolutes, totally beyond our control? Or, are they products of our own attitude, lack of knowledge, and failure to commit and grow? If the latter, then do we mean what we promised, and are we going to do something positive about it? Or, are we going to take the quitters way out, break our promise, and join the divorce statistics?

163

There is no other logical way to look at commitment, as it pertains to marriage. If marriage was easy and effortless, there'd be no need to commit! It isn't easy, it does require effort, it does require change, growth, and knowledge, so we have to commit to it if we are to overcome the challenges. It is totally naive to think any other way. Are we truly committed to the vows we made, and to the marriage we entered... or did we have our fingers crossed behind our back? Did we include the caveat: "...as long as I don't have to learn to relate, communicate, understand, and grow, then I take you as my spouse"? *Did you mean: "I Do?"... Or, "Maybe I Do?"*

Problems?... Or Symptoms?

Have you ever known couples who made comments like: "The little woman hasn't talked to me in weeks, and I'm sick of her," and "He never comes home from work anymore, I might as well be single"? Such comments indicate our widespread confusion between the real problems in our relationships, and the symptoms of the problems. Do you go to the doctor because you're tired of facial tissue, or because you want him to cure your cold? This is a distinction we need to constantly make in our marriage relationship. *Too often, you and I assume that the symptoms are the problems, and we therefore never deal with the real issues.*

Many of the problems we face are common to most, if not all, marriages and relationships. We've already discussed how we often **don't know how to understand, communicate with, and relate effectively** to our spouses. That is a problem for many marriages. Symptoms of this problem can range from undue criticism, fault-finding, nagging, frequent arguments, fights, "claming up" for days without speaking, a poor sex life, becoming engrossed in outside activities or work, to infidelity, separation and divorce. It is not uncommon for one spouse to fault the other for a poor sexual relationship, without realizing that the real problem is lousy communications. *In such instances, we react to the symptoms, and ignore the problem!*

The second greatest <u>problem</u> we face in marriage is **lack of commitment**. This problem carries <u>symptoms</u> of all kinds, ranging from unwillingness to study, grow, and change; to becoming excessively involved in sports or other activities; to fostering destructive associations such as infidelity. Failing to truly commit shows up in practically every aspect of the marriage, resulting in our not doing what we could and should do, and doing things we should not be doing.

Irresponsibility is similar to lacking commitment. I'm saddened to admit that the <u>problem</u> of irresponsibility is much too common among us men, especially! Too many husbands never accept the leadership of their families, and often the wives must assume, by default, roles we should be fulfilling. Other <u>symptoms</u> may be inattention, neglect, unhappiness, and inadequate resources, such as money and time, within our homes. If we men, as the leaders of our families, are not consistently open to both finding and accepting those opportunities to better our marriages and our family's future, we are failing to meet our responsibility as the head of the household! As with commitment, lack of responsibility scatters its symptoms across the entire breadth and scope of our family relationships.

There are many other potential <u>problems</u> for our marriages. Most have their roots in the three discussed above. Some of these secondary problems are a *lack of quality time* to devote to our spouse and children, *inadequate incomes* which create financial stress, *too many outside interests* which compete with our relationship, and *outside associations* with other people which damage our own marriage. For some families, having *too many children, or too many child activities*, than we can realistically afford, may also be a problem. Regardless of which problems we may be challenged with, many of the symptoms can be similar.

<u>Symptoms</u> are fairly common in a marriage, regardless of the specific problems we may face. Many problems can produce a *critical atmosphere* in our home, where nagging and

complaining become the rule. Angry arguments and outright fights reflect our growing *frustrations and discontentment*. For some, *withdrawal* may be a usual response, and the "war of words" may be replaced by the "war of silence." When we are unable to find common ground at home, we may look for it elsewhere, *becoming obsessed with outside people or activities* or our work. Indecision and excuse-making may be signs of frustration and *hopelessness*. Our *lack of sexual satisfaction* is frequently tied to discontentment and poor communication. When a marriage is in serious trouble, *infidelity, separation and ultimately divorce* are obvious indications.

Only by developing the ability to differentiate problems from symptoms, and then doing something positive about the problems, will we justify the vows we made to our loved ones.

When It's Right... It's Great!

As challenging as it may be to create a solid, loving marriage relationship, and as much effort as it will require, *the benefits far outweigh the costs!* For proof, seek out those couples you know of who have outstanding relationships, and ask how they feel about it. With very few exceptions, you'll find they believe it was worth the effort.

Exceptional marriages are founded on genuine communication, understanding, compassion, and compromise. A great marriage is, of course, one where love flourishes, where both people genuinely care about each other, and which provides a supportive environment that allows each to grow as an individual. When these elements exist in abundance in any relationship, you have an atmosphere where both spouses feel fulfilled, content, loved, wanted, needed, useful, and happy. Isn't this what we all want when we marry? What better situation is there to promote good health, ambition, motivation to excel, accountability, integrity, teamwork, and future success? Can there be a better learning and growth environment for our children?

A great marriage relationship is founded on challenges, tackled and solved, together; on growth, together; and on a hopeful future, together! Relationships in crisis tend to focus almost exclusively on the past... who did what to whom. Those going nowhere tend to live primarily in the present, both ignoring the past and the hope for a better tomorrow. But, a sound partnership learns from the past, but doesn't dwell on it. It lives today, and savors it. And, it has hopes and dreams for an even better future, and is working toward it. What more could you want? *When a marriage is right... it's great! And, it's worth the effort!*

What can I Do... To Make It Right?

One suggestion is: *don't be afraid to seek the assistance of a qualified counselor!* When our car won't start, most of us think nothing of taking it to a mechanic. Usually, all it needs are a few minor parts and adjustments, and it's running again. Think similarly of your marriage. When we go to a counselor, we are simply seeking the advice and help of a qualified "mechanic" who specializes in repairing the engine of a relationship. *If you need help to bridge the gaps and get moving again... why not get it?*

Secondly, don't be naive! Don't expect to have a mutually satisfactory marriage without effort! We must be willing to commit and stay committed, learn and keep learning, change and keep changing, grow and keep growing, work and keep working... together! Openness, knowledge, real communications, study, setting and following priorities, accepting responsibility for our attitudes and actions, and having shared goals, are parts of the solution which will lead us to the great relationship we desire. *Possibly the greatest hindrance to having a great marriage is... we don't believe that it's going to take conscious effort and work!*

Marriage is a partnership, not a dictatorship! Wives want and need a participatory voice in the marriage. If we think of our marriage as a business, a family corporation, then the husband and wife are partners, and they share the responsibility for a successful household. A partner needs to have a trusted and respected voice, and an active and creative role, in the business. Each partner also needs to trust and respect the opinions and feelings of the other. Wives have both a right and an obligation to be an equal partner in their marriage and home... but, they should consider the benefits of encouraging their husbands to take the leadership role!

Men, we must be willing to accept a leadership role in our families! Our wives almost universally want us to be leaders. Not by fear, abuse, intimidation, force, violence or other such destructive means... they want us to lead through compassion, emotional strength, intelligence, thoughtfulness, teamwork, by example and with love. This is what responsible leadership is always about, and successful marriages demand responsible leadership from the men. If there is ANY problem in our relationship or home, it is OUR responsibility to do something about it! There is nothing sadder than a family which has money, or other, challenges, and a man who will not sacrifice his own selfish interests to look for, find, and do something about it. Far too many families, wives, and children suffer from the plight of a lazy, selfish, and unambitious man who heads the household!

Realize that crises just mean that change is needed... now! Yogi Berra, former baseball great, said "It ain't over... till it's over." If your marriage isn't over... then it still might be saved, and made great! But, change is needed... now! Why not determine, together, what needs to be changed for the better, in both of you, and get to work changing them... permanently?

Lust may be the result of chemistry, but *real love is the result of deciding to love someone.* Even if you don't feel love toward your spouse right now, you <u>can</u> feel it again, if you want to. When both people *commit* to loving each other, genuinely; then *act* according to that decision; loving *feelings* can follow! What have you got to lose by trying?

Recognize this truth: *your next relationship probably won't be any easier than this one is!* So many times, we end our marriages thinking we're going to find "Mr. or Mrs. Right" and live happily ever after. The fallacy of such thinking is born out by the divorce statistics for second and third time marriages, which are as high or higher than for the first timers. No matter who we marry, you and I must still eventually deal with our own challenges, baggage, hang-ups, and changes... or the next relationship will also be affected by them. The person you remarry will bring their own individual problems to the relationship, and they too must either overcome them or succumb to them. It comes down to this fact: for **any** marriage to work, for any of us, we are going to have to search our souls, deal with our challenges, and make changes within ourselves. If we're going to have to do this anyway... *why not just do it with the one we're married to now?*

You can probably benefit from a learning and self-growth program. Why not start one today, for the rest of your life? Study from the masters how to build and maintain good relationships. Do it together, and you'll grow together. Think what you can teach your children, and how much pain you might spare them. *Don't allow your relationship to suffer from ignorance!*

Learn to Love! Love to Learn! And Begin to Love Life! Together!

CHAPTER NINETEEN
IS YOUR LIFE A SPECTATOR SPORT?

She was a middle-aged housewife, with three school-age children. Every day, she hurried her children off to school so she could watch her four hours of favorite TV shows. After a quick lunch, she would run to the corner store to get the latest tabloid, the reading of which took her till school was out. For the next two to three hours, she raced her children to their various and many activities. As she could fit it in, she would read a romance novel, another daily passion of hers. Following a quick dinner, as the children did their homework, and her husband caught up on his favorite television sports updates, she went back to her novel, before the last two television hours and bedtime. On weekends, they varied little from this routine, except two or three movies each day replaced work and school.

If this example sounds like someone you know, have you wondered how much more they could accomplish if they just managed their time more effectively? In this age of high technology, mass communications, and the glut of not-so-meaningful activities we may indulge in, *we can easily become so engrossed in this "stuff" that life, and success, begin to pass us by.*

Watching Life Go By!

Our lives are precious things, and it is a tragedy anytime a life is lessened! Most of us would automatically think of an early death, when broaching this subject of lessened life. *However, few of us stop to consider how we also waste our lives simply because we don't live them!*

First, let us caveat this section with the obvious truth that we all need a certain amount of recreational and other down time just to relax and charge our mental batteries. You've probably heard the expression that "all work and no play makes Jack a very dull boy." You and I need to have that time and those activities that we enjoy, just for the sake of relaxation. Without this, we become too serious and risk building unhealthy stress loads in our lives. So, we're not talking about degrading this important part of our lives. What we're talking about is whether we're too involved in unproductive activities, and is it costing us both achievement and quality of life? *Balance is almost always a great quality to strive for, and we should consider whether we have the best balance in using our most precious resource... our time (which is also our life!).*

Let's begin with a common interest many of us, guys in particular, may have: *spectator sports, or playing social or organized sports*, such as softball, bowling, or basketball. I personally am a college football fanatic, and I'm not alone. Others may love professional football, hockey, car racing, golf, or dozens of other sports choices. A fanatic for sports, either as a spectator or an intramural participant, could easily spend an <u>extra</u> three hours per week pursuing this passion. This represents only one extra game a week: instead of bowling one night weekly, we bowl twice; or, we watch three games rather than two; for example. While this may not sound like a big deal, have you thought how much time this would total per year? In the average year, this habit would consume nearly one extra week of time. *Over an adult lifespan of fifty years, we could spend over ten months, twenty-four hours a day, just with our excess sports habit!*

Maybe you enjoy movies, videos, video arcades, or computer games? Some people spend dozens of hours weekly in these various activities. Let's assume that someone spends just five hours of <u>excessive</u> time per week doing some or all of these. Over a year, they would tie up nearly eleven full days in front of their screens. *With a fifty year habit, an individual would spend one-and-a-half years of their life watching or playing with these electronic gadgets!*

Perhaps we're an avid fan of recreational reading, such as romance or mystery novels, or tabloids. We could readily devote an <u>extra</u> five or more hours, weekly, sitting with our favorite books or periodicals. *This habit, again, would require another eleven, twenty-four-hour days per year, or eighteen months during our standard fifty year adult life.*

Many of us either have or will have children. *Today's child has a wide array of activities they may participate in!* We can involve our children in numerous different sports, even at an early age. Some may learn dance, ballet, gymnastics, martial arts, swimming, and any number of other hobbies. While we all agree that our youngsters can benefit from learning various skills and disciplines, just how much is too much? Some families seem to have their children in every activity they can find, maybe even pushing their offspring into things they aren't interested in. In such a home, with several children, one or both parents can lead an extremely hectic life, racing child after child to and from various pursuits. A parent who spent an <u>extra</u> ten hours of their week in this manner, would have used about three "around-the-clock" weeks of their time each twelve months. *If their child-rearing time spanned twenty years, this father or mother would devote nearly fourteen months to "running themselves ragged."*

How much sleep do you <u>need</u> every night? Our sleep habits vary considerably from person to person. One may get by very well on five hours of nightly rest, while another feels they need twelve hours at least. We all need a certain amount of daily rest and sleep, in order to stay healthy and function at peak performance. However, it is possible to form a habit of sleeping excessively. In contrast, Benjamin Franklin reportedly found that he needed only four to five hours of nightly sleep. If you're an individual who might have an excess sleep habit, consider the effect of sleeping just one hour longer than needed, each day. *This one extra hour per day would total up to fifteen days per year! Five extra months every decade. Over fifty years of adult life, this additional hour daily would cost two years of awake time. Could you use that time?*

Possibly the greatest drain of all on our non-working time is the television set! Surveys indicate that the average American watches around forty hours of TV each week. Since the vast majority of programming is for entertainment, this time is seldom productive in other ways. Over each fifty-two week period, the average man or woman will watch television the equivalent of three months, twenty-four hours per day. *If this habit was continued over a seventy-year lifespan, it would amount to well over sixteen years in front of the television set!*

If this average person had all these habits to the degree depicted, in his or her seventy year life they would spend nearly twenty-four years of it just in these activities! This is almost one-third of their life, spent in ways that are usually non-productive for the individual concerned.

Ask most people what their biggest challenges are, and you'll frequently hear "money and time." Both these problems are adversely affected by non-productive habits, which, in effect, just waste time. Yet, time (and life) is our most precious non-renewable resource. Once it's gone, it can never be re-claimed. *Any time that you and I waste, or spend non-productively, is life... passing us by!*

Increase Your Life... By Using Your Time More Productively!

In today's hectic world, most of us feel we need more time! The most overworked excuse is "... but, I just don't have the time." Likewise, there are few people who don't want or need more spendable money. If you can relate to this, how would you like to do something positive about both challenges? You can, just by managing your time for more productivity.

Most of us waste our time when we have no real purpose for using it! Without dreams, goals, and a vision for where we want our lives to go, our ambition and motivation are usually lacking. Having no ambition or motivation leads to spending great amounts of time in pursuit of entertainment or pleasure, rather than in more positive ways. You should seriously consider thinking about your vision or definite major purpose for living. Determine what you want your time on this earth to mean, to stand for, what you truly want to accomplish. From this overall purpose, you can then create specific goals for taking you down the path of your definite major purpose. Goals will help you create daily habits which can keep you moving toward your vision.

Would you like to have an extra day every month, just to focus on the goal-oriented habits you want to create, and to do those things which improve yourself and your life? This can be done by taking a close look at how you now use your time. Learning to cut out some of your current activities which are non-productive, can help you begin to "buy back" some of your life. *If you could find just one extra hour per day, and make positive use of it, this would net you over one extra day each month, fifteen days per year, and five months each decade.*

We rarely use non-productive time. One such example is traveling or commuting time in a vehicle. If one of your goals is to create a self-growth reading and motivation program, could you put commuting time to use for this? If you use public transportation, could you spend a half-hour to an hour each day, reading a self-improvement book? Or listening to a motivational or inspirational tape, if you drive yourself? Coffee breaks and lunch hours could be used in similar ways, in many instances. *If you scrutinized your time in detail, chances are you could find at least one wasted hour each day, which could be used more effectively. Using what is now a wasted hour, daily, would give you another day monthly, fifteen days more each year, and five months every decade... to put to constructive use!*

Perhaps you could make established habits more productive instead of just entertaining. An example might be reading. If you now read tabloids, novels, or periodicals on a daily basis, it would be possible to reduce this recreational reading, and read instead from books which can enhance your business knowledge, personal growth, or motivation, for example. In effect, you would just be substituting a more productive and goal-oriented habit for a portion of one which had little long-term value.

Our children are an important priority, and they should be exposed to those activities which can help them develop, physically and emotionally. *However, there is a limit to what a child needs, or can absorb, or to what is financially prudent within a family's budget constraints.* In addition, children need to spend quality time with their parents, and involving them in too many outside activities may be detrimental in that regard. Given these considerations, some of us may have our children more involved in various programs than is wise or necessary. And, many varied activities can simply dominate parents' time management! If this relates to you, perhaps a fresh evaluation would be in order. Reducing or eliminating some activities may benefit your child by allowing them to focus their interests in one specific area where they show the most aptitude or talent, give them more quality time with you, and let them have more time to just play. Also, it could still potentially yield an extra hour or two for you to devote to <u>your</u> other needs.

With regard to our children, we all should remember one fact as we dole out our time. *Our children, yours and mine, are only temporary visitors in our homes!* Sooner or later, they grow up and move out on their own. We need to remember this for two reasons: one, so we will savor and cherish the time we do have them and use it fully; and, two, so we make time for ourselves, as husbands and wives. *We cannot afford to neglect our marriage relationship, because one day we will still have to share an otherwise empty house with each other!*

There are numerous time management resources which can help us be more productive. Just a simple notebook to keep track of our priorities and obligations is a good start. For more complicated situations, one may use a daily planning system. These allow us to not only list our time needs, but prioritize and check off tasks as each is accomplished. Self-help books offer excellent advice and insight for using our time more wisely and effectively.

In the final analysis, if you were to establish a ***clear purpose*** for your future, and then ***prioritize*** your resulting goals, you would gain a better idea of how you needed to *budget* your time. Should you then be willing to find and use some previously unproductive time, you could potentially chip away at some of the current challenges you face, or work at improving yourself and your success potential.

Time is our single most critical resource! If you feel like a spectator to your own life, evaluate how you now spend your time, prioritize accordingly, manage effectively, and... buy back a major part of your life to put to more productive use!

CHAPTER TWENTY
RUNNING ON EMPTY... FROM LACK OF FAITH?

Everything looked very good to Bill! He had checked this new job offer thoroughly, and received very competent advice which was quite encouraging. He'd always wanted a shot at the top, and this looked like just what he needed. But, the more he thought about it, the more he pulled back. Bill was not well educated, and had never been in such a business before. The job would involve people, and he had never been comfortable dealing with strangers. There were dozens of other questions, too. He just wasn't sure he could handle the demands. Anyway, he'd accomplished almost nothing so far in his 35 years of life, why should he expect to now?

Have you ever found yourself in Bill's situation? Was there ever a time when you lacked confidence in your abilities to succeed? Have you just found yourself on what seems to be a dead-end road, going nowhere in life, and with no light at the end of the tunnel? If these relate all-too-well to you, perhaps what you're really short of... is faith! We'll try to illuminate this feeling of running in quicksand, when we're running on empty... from lack of faith!

What Is This Thing Called "Faith"?

Mention faith to most people, and they'll have some intuitive idea of what we're talking about, often based on religious connotations. However, faith can apply to far more than just religious faith, although this may be its most important application. The dictionary tells us that "faith" has three common meanings. The first is an "unquestioning belief" (often associated with "God"). It may also mean having "complete trust and confidence" in something or someone; or it can mean "loyalty" to a person or concept. For our purposes, all three meanings may apply, but the emphasis is on the first two. *So, what we'll be discussing is a state of having* **"unquestioning belief in; trust and confidence in; or loyalty to"** *a concept or entity.*

Give thought to this definition, and you'll realize that we are talking about an intangible *state of mind*, and not a tangible thing! Faith is not something we can pick up, touch, taste, smell, or hear. It is a feeling we have which stems from an attitude of positive belief. Faith is literally the opposite of doubt and fear. Since doubt, fear, worry, and cynicism live in a negative mental attitude, it follows, then, that *faith can only exist in a mind which is positive!*

Faith is a gift! Faith is a feeling that may come, if it comes, from consciously nurturing an environment favorable to its growth. While we may choose to trust, we cannot simply choose to have faith. We can only choose to create the personal conditions which may promote faith.

We can only observe the outward signs, or manifestations, of faith, not faith itself. One's faith in a divine Creator is only evident from the way they live their life, from the love and charity they exhibit, from how they spend their time and money. *What we actually "do" gives definition to our real "faith."*

The Emptiness that comes from Lacking Faith!

There are four main areas in which we may have, or not have, faith. On the most personal level, you and I should have faith in *ourselves*. We can, and should, have belief in our abilities, our character, our strengths, our inner powers which carry us through adversity and toward success in life. We can also believe in *what we do*, both to earn a living and to make a difference in the world. Regardless of our income level or social status, we can have faith and belief that the services we provide are decent, honorable and of relative value to humanity. No matter who we are or what we do, we need to trust and believe in other *people*. We need to believe that people in general, and certain people in particular, will live up to our trust, confidence, and expectations. And, of course, nearly all of us will eventually come to conceptual terms with *a greater purpose, a reason for being, a divine guidance, a source of*

***universal intelligence and power... which many know as
"God."***

*The man or woman who lacks faith in themselves lives in a
mental state of self-doubt.* Unsure of themselves, lacking
confidence in their abilities and decisions, while not believing
anything will change for the better, fear freezes them into
inaction. This individual undoubtedly has worry as their
constant companion. Although they may even lack the
confidence to complain, their state of mind can only be
characterized as negative. They go through the motions of life,
doing what they know how to do, and not expecting anything to
improve. They are the epitome of those who "live lives of quiet
desperation"!

*We define our lives by the things we do! To feel fulfilled, we
must believe in the value and worthiness of our life's work.*
Many of us are involved in organizations, sports, and hobbies
which further refine and emphasize who we are. Whatever we
do with our lives, we have the same basic needs for reward,
recognition, accomplishment, creativity, expression, belonging,
acceptance, and a sense of worthy contribution to other people.
If our work does not satisfy those needs, adequately, then we
have a feeling of going nowhere in life.

Some of us will choose an occupation or profession which, in
our youth, appears to be everything we're seeking. Yet, as we
mature and age, our satisfaction and sense of meaningful
accomplishment diminishes to the point that we find ourselves
"burned out" and wishing for a change years before we can
afford to retire. This situation is fertile ground for growing a
negative attitude which prohibits faith. Lacking faith that our
efforts make the difference we wanted, our loyalty and
commitment dwindle, work becomes drudgery, and our time
seems to just waste away with little to show for it.

People play a part in our lives, regardless of what we do for a
living! Family, friends, and acquaintances affect us virtually
every day of our existence. *We must believe there is intrinsic*

good in all people. Some, however, develop habits, character traits, and lifestyles which are mediocre, not-so-good, and a few downright evil. On a personal level, we know people who, in positive or negative ways, may inspire, motivate, educate, advise, and otherwise influence us. We judge others based partly upon our past experiences, and our faith or lack of faith, in people, will usually reflect our experiences and perceptions.

If we have no faith in people, we will become cynical, distrust the motives of even those closest to us, be reluctant to believe what anybody says, and expect them to be deceitful, self-serving and unworthy. We tend to avoid close relationships, ignore advice and counsel, reject offers to help us, sometimes take advantage of or hurt others, and generally expect to make it in life on our own. In essence, we become loners... when we lack faith in people!

Many people will eventually feel an emptiness, that "something" is missing, if they have no faith in a universal power greater than themselves! At some times in our lives, we need to sense that we are part of the greater whole; that we function in an ordered and structured universe. And, as we begin to understand the awesome magnificence of just our earth, the more we may need a purpose greater than self-interest; to connect with an intelligence and power greater than ourselves; to sense universal knowledge and truth. Some of us may grasp a higher calling, everyday guidance, and our sense of right and wrong from this relationship.

Whatever one may call this, Infinite Intelligence, the Creator, Divine Guidance, or God, there can be no doubt that it is a source of personal strength for many around the world. For those who sense <u>no</u> such power, who <u>do not</u> connect with any purpose beyond themselves, they base their entire life on <u>personal</u> resources and interests only. Their tendency is to live on the expediency of the present with little concern for the future. If we lack faith in any power and purpose beyond our individual self, it leads to self-centeredness, selfishness, aloofness, egotism, and vanity. The passing years ultimately produce feelings of emptiness, loneliness, and lack of fulfillment.

Finally, if we lack faith, we will find it difficult to take positive action! We need to be <u>motivated</u> in order to change anything for the better. However, motivation comes from a combination of at least two sources. One of these sources is what we want to achieve: ***our wants, needs, desires, dreams.*** Without something significant to do, or to achieve, or to become, or to give... we will have no motivation to act! Likewise, the second element of motivation is ***faith or belief*** that we can accomplish what we wish to accomplish! If we do not believe that we can achieve our dream or goal, then we also have no motivation to act! I can constantly dream of owning a new cadillac automobile, but if I don't believe I will ever own one, then I'll have no motivation to take any realistic steps toward obtaining a cadillac. *Without faith that we may achieve them, our dreams and goals are nothing more than wishful thinking!*

Lacking faith is like living in a house without doors, at the mercy of circumstances, with dwindling hope for fulfilling our desires and dreams, whatever they may be!

The Power of Faith!

As stated before, faith is the opposite of doubt and fear, and can therefore only exist with a positive mental attitude. And, when faith is present in a mind which is positive, the resulting power is perhaps one of our least understood and most under-estimated resources!

Those who believe in themselves have faith that what they desire to achieve, they can in fact do! They have confidence in their own abilities, trust that they can succeed with sincere and concerted effort, and believe they are worthy of achieving. They have dreams and goals that they intend to reach; and see past mistakes and defeats as only temporary stepping-stones and learning experiences to propel themselves toward greater potential. In short, the individual who has faith in himself or herself functions in a mental state oriented toward success and progress.

Similarly, the fortunate soul who believes in what they do has a superior advantage over one who does not. Confident that their efforts make a positive difference, both for themselves and for others; and that it is decent, honest, and moral work; they are easily committed to what they're doing. Unlike so many other unhappy laborers, this character is eager to work because they know they're doing the right thing. The positive faith behind their effort makes them highly creative, effective, and productive!

Other people represent a limitless supply of support, wisdom, and guidance to the one who recognizes and develops it in a thoughtful, caring, and faith-filled way. Having faith in people, that many do care and will give us the best they have to offer, helps us unlock the door to this resource. Mature faith is not gullible, it acknowledges that some are unworthy of our confidence. However, mature faith knows that many are worthy, and we just need to apply common sense and open-mindedness as we allow others to earn our trust.

Lastly, in the broadest sense, when we have faith in a universal power we tap a source of strength and creativity which is a primary factor in most, if not all, miracles. It may also become a source of divine guidance in our everyday lives. To Christians this is God. *With such belief, we have a greater purpose for our lives and grasp a more self-less reason for being on this planet.* Tuned in to the "still, small voice" that talks to us from within, we may gain insight, wisdom, knowledge, and a sense of morality and righteousness which are foreign to those who have no such relationship. The human being who comprehends, embraces, and is blessed with faith in a higher, universal power, has discovered a reservoir of truth, natural law, and inspiration which is infinite!

How May I Nurture Faith?

If you feel that faith may be lacking in your life, study and contemplate this concept until you understand that it can prevent you from having the life you want. Then, begin a conscious program to develop faith. *Realize that faith is a quality which may be cultivated by creating a positive environment to promote its development!*

Faith can only live in a mind which is positive! It is the exact opposite of doubt and fear, which flourish in a negative mental attitude. Therefore, the challenge you must tackle is that of overall attitude. The mental environment we must foster is that of positive, creative thinking. Good things, including faith, will only come from a positive attitude!

Recognize that faith, by itself, will result in nothing! The other component of motivation is that of want. We have to want something in order to be motivated to do whatever effort it requires. So, you would be wise to re-discover what you want, need, and desire from life... re-kindle your dreams; and set goals for achieving them. Create a vision for your life. *Faith, and motivation, will come easier to those who have a definite purpose, an overall vision, and an absolute desire to achieve it.*

Inventory your assets, abilities, and resources, including the ability to think logically, living in a free nation, the benefits of a free enterprise economic system, the freedom to make choices, the freedom to change, and others. You'll undoubtedly conclude that you have all the resources you need to achieve and become anything you want! When we are blessed with freedom, we are able to become better than we are now. We are free to pursue our dreams! *Convince yourself that, with these tools on your team, and the willingness to work and persist, you have what it takes to grow and succeed!*

Weigh the advantages and attributes of what you do for a living, and whom you associate with. If you don't have faith in what you do or in other people, perhaps this is holding you back. You might need to reconsider your occupation. Negative associations may be hurting your "success potential." It could be necessary for you to consider making changes in one or both areas. Remain aware that there are occupations and people that you can believe in and be fulfilled with... you just need to find them! Why "settle for" less than you want? Go after it!

Review those areas where your faith is lacking, and consider becoming a student of them. *Be open-minded to learning and becoming more.* As you seek the truth, facts, knowledge, and wisdom in that specific part of your life, you will gain greater insight and confidence which may nourish faith. Understand that, ultimately, you can only influence real faith by influencing the environment which is most favorable to it. Faith itself is a gift which either is, or is not. Create a positive atmosphere, and pray that it becomes filled with faith.

Understand that faith must be active, not passive*, if it is to be of value!* This is because faith is a state of mind, and can only be expressed through action. Faith manifests itself through our words, our actions, our habits, our deeds, our work, and eventually through our character. If we want to have faith, in anything, we must begin to think, talk, act, and live... as if we already have that faith. Positive actions not only express the feelings we want, but they help those feelings to grow. The Bible sums it up simply: "faith, without works, is dead"!

"What the mind of man can conceive and believe, the mind of man can achieve." (Napoleon Hill)

"Deep faith eliminates fear." (Franklin Delano Roosevelt)

"For we walk by faith, not by sight." (II Corinthians 5:7)

"Faith is the best path to freedom."
(Pope John Paul; 1998. Statement during visit to Cuba.)

CHAPTER TWENTY-ONE
IS RELIGION YOUR EXCUSE... FOR FAILING?

There are many differing perspectives and interpretations on the subject of religious faith. Many people around the world feel and display a visibly passionate faith in a divine Creator. Some have a quiet but strong religious faith. Others are somewhat neutral, perhaps not knowing for sure what they believe. And, there are those who do not believe at all in divine creation. My hope is that the reader will take this chapter for the perspective it offers. Just as you don't buy everything in the grocery store, each time you shop, neither do you have to buy everything, or anything, that I've presented. Perhaps, though, I may invigorate your thinking in this area. If so, great!

Let's first admit that the subjects of religion and faith are sensitive ones, mostly because they are so personal to each one of us. They are personal because *" religious faith" is an abstract concept, a gift of unconditional belief in a higher power, that comes from within!* Being abstract, we cannot see, hear, touch, taste, or smell faith. Faith by itself, is a <u>passive</u> quality because it is a state of mind which cannot be seen, challenged, proven, or disproved. We can only sense someone's faith by what they say, and observing what they do over time. In that regard, faith may also be an <u>active</u> quality. *Indeed, real faith is always active faith, for it will reflect itself in our thoughts, words, deeds, actions, habits, and in the way we live.*

Since nobody can challenge us on what we say are our religious beliefs, and because we may have difficulty grasping them fully ourselves, it is possible to allow our religion and our faith to be used as an excuse! As with any excuse, we thereby justify doing what we should not be doing; or not doing what we should or could do. Making excuses, for any reason, is one of the attitudes which prevents us from realizing our full potential.

How do we know if we are using our religion or faith as an excuse to justify actions or decisions in God's name? Are we following divine guidance? Or, are we just doing what we want to do? Are we simply validating the easier choices, an unwillingness to change? Since I am not an expert on religions or the Bible, this discussion will be based upon my limited understanding of God's word. It will, however, reflect my comprehension of the truth, as best I understand it. My goal is to stimulate you to consider a reasoned insight into this important part of our lives. First, let's find some common ground.

Religion? Or, Faith?

When we talk about religious faith, we all understand that we are discussing "an unconditional belief in a divine power" (*"God"* for much of the world). This faith is common to all who believe in a higher power, regardless of their religion or denomination. Christians, Jews, Muslims, Buddhists, and others all share faith in a higher power. As we transition to *religion*, though, we consider more humanly characteristics. The definition of religion which most applies in this context is "a specific system of belief or worship, built around God, a code of ethics, or a philosophy of life." For our discussion, *"religion" refers to those systems which man has developed in order to exercise and demonstrate his faith in a higher, universal power (which we Christians know as "God").* Christianity, Islam, Buddhism, Catholicism, Mormonism, and so on, all qualify as religions, in this context. As human creations, religions are subject to human conditions and interpretations.

Religious faith is an absolute! We either believe, or we don't believe, in a higher, universal power. One may pretend to believe, and might even fool most others into thinking we're genuine believers, but we seldom fool ourselves. We still know if we believe, or not. As discussed in the previous chapter, faith is a state of mind which may be nourished, even if one doesn't have it right now. Many of us don't acquire real religious faith until well into our lives.

On the other hand, our religion is not absolute! We can change from one religion to another, or to different denominations within a major religion. A Catholic can change and become a Buddhist; a Baptist can join the Lutheran Church, and so on. Our religious beliefs can be open to a wide range of interpretations. Especially when dealing with such abstract and deeply personal subjects as prayer, and our relationship with God, the interpretations and conclusions can be very diverse and difficult to totally define or describe. Unless we subscribe to accurate thinking, we can even fake ourselves out.

Are We Making Excuses?

Have you ever known someone who justified their action or inaction because "God told me so"? Or, because "I don't need to do anything more; God will provide"? Have you wondered if they really meant what they said? Or, were they just making excuses because they didn't want to do something different or challenging? One thing we know for sure: *a person who makes excuses, for any reason, to avoid doing the difficult but right things and to avoid the hard but necessary choices, is a person who will prevent himself or herself from reaching their greatest potential!* For this reason, and because faith is an abstract quality which can be used to make excuses, we will attempt to reason together on this delicate issue.

A key question is this: "does God make us do things"? In particular, "does God tell us what to do in the routine decisions affecting our lives"? Or, are we provided **guidance**, through written documents, through our sense of right and wrong, and through prayer, with which to make our own best decisions? For example, "should I invest in this, or not"? Assuming both are honest, legal, and honorable options, this is not an issue of right versus wrong, it's an issue of what's best, considering the circumstances. In such a decision, can we expect God to tell us what to do? Or, does He expect us to weigh all the factors in light of His guidance about family, responsibility, prosperity, striving for excellence, and doing the right thing... and make the decision that's best in our situation? Does He provide guidance, or give orders?

The crucial consideration, in seeking an answer to this question, is that of decision, or choice. Who has the power to decide? Is God making our decisions for us? Or, are we making the decisions? The answer seems obvious: we have the choice! The decision is ours. In the example above, it would be my choice whether to invest or not. As a man, husband, and father, I must consider my needs and abilities, my family's needs, and all other pertinent factors, then make the decision which is best. God guides me, but gives me the choice.

How does God guide us? For Christians, this answer is in the Bible. The Bible is perhaps the greatest book on successful and worthy living ever written! Other religions have their equivalent to the Bible. In them, we receive instruction on how to live good, honorable, and worthwhile lives. The Ten Commandments of Christianity tell us to live within certain standards of human decency, not stealing, murdering, committing adultery, and so forth. In other scripture, we are instructed to prosper in all ways, to live and work well, to love our spouses with honor, to honor our parents, and on and on. And, we may tie into the Source of universal power through the power of prayer. Using these resources, we are abundantly equipped to make our own proper and best choices! With these tools, we have the decision-making capability to live rewarding, honorable and prosperous lives, as He obviously intended for us!

Should you need further convincing, look to the histories of the Middle East, Ireland, Bosnia, the United States, and many other nations. Observe the crime, inhumanity, and atrocities committed against one another, often in the name of religious conviction. Innocent men, women, and children are maimed or killed in horrible ways, every day, too often by those claiming divine authority. Would any just and loving God direct us to do such terrible things to each other... if He were making our decisions for us?

Specifically, if we reject opportunities to potentially better our lives, or improve the lives of our loved ones who depend upon us, with the reasoning that "God told me not to," aren't we making excuses? If we truly research God's word in the Bible, there is plenty of evidence that He wants us to succeed and prosper, not live in poverty of spirit, character, or pocketbook. And, as we've been rationalizing, we have been given the freedom to choose that which is best, voluntarily. No higher power makes these decisions for us. *To indicate that God chose for us, is to either lie, or make an excuse, or both.*

There can be no other logical conclusion! God has given us direction in how to live worthy. He makes it clear that we are expected to succeed in life, not just drift through it without meaningful accomplishment and purpose. We have the resources to direct our own lives, including the freedom to make our own choices. God has provided this for us.

God <u>Has</u> Provided!

There is a humorous story, resulting from the terrible floods in the American mid-west during the 1990's, which gives us pause to reflect on this issue. In this story, a homeowner is stranded in his house as the flood waters are rising rapidly all around him. As he stands on his front porch in ankle-deep water, a rowboat pulls up to him. The man in the boat yells at the fellow to get in and escape before the waters take his house. Our homeowner, though, calmly replies that "God will provide for me; pick up the people in the other houses." Shortly thereafter, now from the roof of his porch, again in ankle-deep water, our gentleman is hailed by the driver of a speedboat to climb in and be taken to safety. Again, our man replies that "God will provide; get someone else who needs a ride worse than I do."

Not long after this, the owner is now on the peak of his roof, as water threatens to completely engulf his house. From the rainy skies, a helicopter beckons him to grab the ladder and climb aboard. Still, he declines the offer for rescue, saying

"God will provide, get somebody else." Within minutes, our faithful servant is swept from his roof and drowns. As his soul waits before God for check-in to heaven, he asks God, "God, I always thought you'd look after me and provide for me. Why was it, that you let me drown?" God replied "I sent you two boats and a helicopter! What more did you expect me to do?"

Aside from this humorous anecdote, if you and I truly reflect upon all our blessings, we can only conclude that God already *has provided* for us! We have been provided with three of the greatest assets, available only to the human species. One asset is that we have the most complex and advanced brain of any creature on this planet. We have the ability, within the vast network of our brain cells, **to reason and think logically** in abstract terms. Secondly, we have been given complete **freedom of choice** in how we use our minds, what and how we think, and the power of decision. And, we have been given **dominion** over all other creatures of this earth. With these resources provided to each and every one of us at birth, we are completely capable of taking care of ourselves. We are already provided for!

Some would have us believe that our path is charted at birth. This theory says that everything we do, every step we take, is part of a divine plan. This theory, however, is not logical. For one reason, why would we have the assets noted above, if we were going to be moved through a divine plan like so many chess pieces? Why wouldn't a Creator just make us as another beast, bird, or fish, and let us only concern ourselves with survival? We'd be much easier to control! Besides that, how do we explain the horrible things that we do to each other? Can we possibly believe that a good God would willingly program us to murder, rape, and torture? Or, to be a victim of such crimes? Especially when those crimes are against our youngest and most innocent children? Since this theory is not logical, then we must consider that we have been given the freedom to choose what we do, right from wrong, good from evil.

Can there be another logical or Biblical conclusion, except that we have the freedom of choice? In all issues, great and small, good versus evil, right or wrong, you and I have the power of decision... God doesn't decide for us. Yes, we have inherited much guidance on how to properly live productive and worthwhile lives. Yet, with every instruction, we, individually, have freedom of choice. Even the Ten Commandments, which we are directed to follow, are up to each of us to voluntarily honor. The fact that murder, adultery, rape, torture, and other crimes occur, every day, undeniably proves these are OUR choices. Even the devil doesn't make us do these awful things. The devil may tempt us... but, we choose to follow, or not!

In Christianity, the defining event is the death and resurrection of Jesus. In our faith, this was the ultimate step to offer all of humanity the greatest of all gifts: redemption from sin, and eternal salvation. The Bible tells us, as Christians, we have only to accept Christ as our savior, and we are saved from eternal damnation by the grace of God. Yet, even this greatest of all offerings... is still left up to our individual decision! Each of us, as individuals, must voluntarily make this decision and accept His grace. *Why would God leave this most important decision to our free will and choice, yet make our lesser decisions for us?* This is exactly what you and I would have others believe, when we justify our actions with words to the effect, "God made me do (or not do) this thing"!

Through prayer, we have the ability to tap that source of universal truth and power, which we Christians call "God." Whatever name our beliefs place on this resource, it is a source of personal guidance and strength for millions around the globe. It is considered a large component, perhaps "the" component, from which miracles occur. The relationship, or lack of relationship, that we have with divine guidance and universal intelligence through prayer... is each person's responsibility to develop at the most personal level.

The guidance we receive from prayer is sometimes described as the "still, small voice" that speaks to us from within the depths of our subconscious minds. As with any thought that comes by way of our subconscious, we have the conscious choice whether to act on it or not. We have received ample Biblical guidance instructing us how to live meaningful and fruitful lives. Within the context of such guidance, our conscience and, through prayer, our subconscious (the "still, small voice from within"!) act as the rudder of a great ship, allowing us to stay on course.

*From this perspective, then, the underlying thread is **freedom of choice!*** This is perhaps God's greatest gift to us, because it opens the door to every treasure this life has to offer, and to salvation when life has ended. With freedom of choice, all of our decisions become our own. We cannot place their burden upon anyone else, including God. And, He has given us the complete control of our minds and therefore of our thoughts and dreams and ambitions. *He wants us to amount to something; to reach our full potential, and to do so out of love, voluntarily, because we want to and choose to!* This is how He has provided for us.

If you, the reader, accepts this perspective, then you must also accept that you are responsible for your life, and for how you use it! If you are to eat, you must feed yourself. If you are to prosper, you must find the way and work to do so. If your children are to go to college, you are responsible for helping them. If you are unfaithful to your spouse, you are the one who must make the change to become faithful. If the earth is to remain a fit place for our children and their children, then it is up to us to keep it so. And, on and on, ad infinitum. *We have been given the tools and all the resources we need... it's up to us to benefit from them, to provide for ourselves!*

"A noble and Godlike character is not a thing of favor or chance, but is the natural result of continued effort in right thinking, the effect of long-cherished association with Godlike thoughts. An ignoble and bestial character, by the same process, is the result of the continued harboring of groveling thoughts." (James Allen, *As a Man Thinketh*)

Faith, and prayer, can help us find the answers we seek. But, it is still up to us to accept those answers, accept our responsibilities, and act upon both.

CHAPTER TWENTY-TWO
SUFFERING FROM "TALK-ITIS,"
THE MOUTH DISEASE?

She was a small town girl with big time dreams! Angela was well read, could recite volumes from many success oriented authors, and she was particularly well versed in the Bible. She loved to talk, and would pass up no opportunity to discuss heavy subjects. The town was holding her back, she said, and she needed to be in a place where she could blossom and make her mark. Opportunities came her way, from people who were impressed with what she said. Angela rejected them, though, because she intended to start up her own new company. However, months later she still talked big, yet was not doing what she claimed to want to do.

Have you ever had a friend who seemed to always have the answers, and told you so? Regardless of the topic, they usually had extensive opinions to share, and generally had the last word? After a time, didn't you start to question both their wisdom and their commitment, since few things ever changed for them? Most of us know people like this, who talk big, but seldom do anything. Here, we'll think about *"talk-itis,"* or *"talking a good show,"* and consider it's effect if we don't back it up with action.

Great Intentions! "Someday I'm gonna... "

As with all the topics we're discussing, there is a pattern to the guy or gal who is more talk than action. This pattern centers around great intentions! The person we're referring to always has the best of intentions to do this or that. You could even name this syndrome something like the *"Someday, I'm gonna... " syndrome*. Someday I'm gonna win the lottery; someday I'm gonna start my own business; someday I'm gonna run for mayor; someday I'm gonna have it all; someday... someday... someday. Some may be more creative, and use variations like "I intend to... "; "Just as soon as I have the money... "; "As soon as I have the time... "; "Once this big deal comes through... "; etc., etc. There is only one problem: "someday" just never seems to get here!

Why are some People All Talk?

The *"someday I'm gonna... " syndrome* seems, at first glance, like unaccountability, since people say they're going to do things, but never seem to get them done. That would over-simplify this particular trait, though, because the underlying factors probably run deeper than just lack of discipline. In the "someday I'm gonna" person, their lack of accountability is more to themselves than to someone else.

You're possibly familiar with the game of verbally outdoing the other person. This is often referred to as "one-upping" the other's story or comment. For those individuals who are afflicted by talk-itis, there is a need to somehow outdo, with words, whoever they may be talking with. This individual must come away from their verbal exchanges feeling that they had the most to say, the best things to say, the last word, or in some way won the encounter. This need for verbal one-up-manship with other people is related to the "someday I'm gonna... " syndrome in that both satisfy the talker's need to bolster their ego.

The person who suffers from talk-itis uses their own words to satisfy a feeling of personal inadequacy. This individual may actually <u>need</u> to hear themselves sound as if they're intelligent, wise, in control, going somewhere... whether they are, or not. Why would that be? Two probable reasons are lack of confidence and low self-esteem.

The individual who lacks confidence usually feels inadequate and tends to fall short of their potential. They may compare themselves unfavorably to others. Feeling less worldly, less wise, less educated, less successful, than many of those whom they associate with, our person may over-compensate in other areas in order to seem confident. An easy way is to pretend to be self-assured, to talk as if we know what we're talking about and as if we're "moving on" in life! Hence, the talk-itis syndrome becomes a substitute for actual ability and success, by talking as if we have the qualities and potential that we actually believe we lack. In short, *talk-itis makes us seem more important, despite the fact that we don't feel very important!*

Similarly, low self-esteem, caused by any number of factors, may give the same result. Regardless of how life has treated us in the past, we all have the basic <u>need</u> to feel good about ourselves. When our self-worth is low, we don't feel deserving of the finer things in life, including success. However, we all have an ego which wants to be deserving. To rectify this dilemma, an easy fix, again, is to <u>talk</u> as though success is just around the corner (though, in our minds we *know* we can't turn that corner!). *The sound of our own words becomes the sedative which dulls the pain of believing we're on the road to nowhere.*

Another reason for talk-itis, the habit of talking but not doing, can be summed up with the wisdom: *talk is cheap!* Virtually everyone can <u>talk</u> about doing, having, giving, and becoming. Talk simply requires the formulation of thoughts and the creation of words to voice those thoughts. Talking is a far cry from doing! <u>Doing</u> what we say involves belief, faith, a plan, commitment, effort, and persistence. Even a person who lacks some or all of these qualities, and who knows he isn't going to actually do something, is still capable of talking as if he intends to do something. In a way, talk-itis is a game of pretend. *Using our words, we are pretending to be motivated, self-assured, capable, and worthy... when in fact, we don't believe we're any of those things!*

Come on now! What's the Harm in just Talking?

Some would say that we need people who are mostly hot air; otherwise, who'd run for political office?

Even when a talker isn't challenged directly on what they say, it is still quite obvious to other people when a person is more talk than action. All it takes is a little time to see if their efforts match their intentions. Once it is apparent that they seldom do, the listener is safe to assume they rarely will. As people begin to judge us as "all talk and no action," our credibility and believability plummet.

If you and I are more talk than action, it erodes our credibility with other people. Perhaps the greatest damage from talking a good show is that the very people who know us best, are the ones who know we aren't credible! So, the talker not only destroys his credibility with those who know him superficially, but he is almost completely unbelievable to those who know and perhaps even love him. Consider the effect that being a talker for many years could have upon your spouses or children. After years of listening to us talk, but not seeing us do anything to support it, wouldn't they eventually stop taking us seriously? If our spouse and children don't take us seriously or believe in us, how effective can we be as a leader in our family? What are we as a man or woman, if we don't have credibility? If our own family doesn't believe what we say, how can we believe in ourselves?

Belief in ourselves is a large part of our own self-esteem and confidence. If it becomes common knowledge that we're just a bunch of hot air, it doesn't take long for us to sense our diminished stature. Since we don't take ourselves very seriously either, we continue to lower our self-worth. Poor self-esteem will be even more of a problem for us as we have less believability and credibility with the people around us!

The Bible says that faith, without works, is dead! Throughout all of mankind's history, never has one word resulted in a tangible and significant achievement... without somebody taking action. The Eiffel Tower was not built by words, it was built with tools and steel in the hands of man. The same with the Tower of London, the Empire State Building, the Golden Gate Bridge, Mount Rushmore, the car you drive and the house you live in. All the talk in the world never felled one tree, never nailed one board, never mortared one brick, and never created one business. Only *commitment and effort* create the substance of our human existence!

It has been my experience that there are "talkers," and there are "do-ers"! The man or woman who has to tell the world of their good intentions, probably has no intention of doing much. Conversely, the person who gets things done is usually too busy doing to take time to talk about it. The person who is confident and self-assured, and who has the guts, gumption and grit to do what they need to do... doesn't have to say much. *Their actions speak for themselves!*

"The world is moving so fast these days that the man who says it can't be done is generally interrupted by someone doing it." (Elbert Hubbard)

How do I Cure "Talk-itis"?

As with everything in this book, recognizing a problem is the first step to doing something constructive about it! Since talk-itis is just another bad habit with underlying causes, then we can work on positively changing both the causes and the habit.

With the habit of talking a good show, but not backing it up with action, we are hurting our chances for long-term success in all areas of importance! We are killing our credibility with those people who are most capable of supporting our goals and dreams. People cannot support us unless they believe in us and find us worthy of their assistance. Talk-itis, therefore, becomes a mind and attitude habit which holds us back. *So, we need to overcome the factors which lead us to the habit.*

Realize that good intentions, alone, don't accomplish anything! Words, without faith and action, are meaningless. While it may be easy to talk about doing or becoming something, the proof is in the pudding. The way we follow-up our talk with work is what counts. Don't kid yourself into thinking other people don't notice the disparity when our actions disprove our words. They do notice! Don't allow talk-itis to weaken your credibility with others. They will believe you, when they see you back up what you say with effort.

Low self-confidence and low self-esteem are likely candidates for causing this disease of the mouth. I'd suggest you re-read chapter two of this book again. Then, begin a program of motivational, inspirational, and self-improvement reading to build your personal foundation of self-worthiness. A few excellent resources are listed in the bibliography. Begin with these, and create a lifelong habit of studying to improve yourself. You'll be amazed at the changes for the better!

What we actually do is a far more powerful persuader, than what we say we're going to do!

Talk is cheap! Action and persistent effort are what always have, and always will, make the difference!

"I wish I could be half as sure of anything as some people are of everything." (Gerald Barzan)

"Nobody wants his cause near as bad as he wants to talk about his cause." (Will Rogers)

CHAPTER TWENTY-THREE
UNSURE IF YOU'RE INDECISIVE?

Doug had a wife and a small son. He was a mid-level professional, and his wife worked as well. Between them, they made enough money for a decent living, but weren't saving like they needed for either education or retirement. For supplemental income, he had a part-time job several nights a week. A friend, one day, offered him a chance to diversify into a part-time business which had considerable potential. It looked like what Doug needed, and he eagerly began to check it out. Time after time, he met with his friend and asked question upon question, seeking more information. A month went by, then another and another. Before long, a year had passed, and still Doug expressed an interest, but always needed to know more. However, he seemed to devote more time to playing basketball than to making a decision. Finally, his friend gave up on him, and began to look for another partner. Doug still worked at his same jobs, two years later.

Diane lived in a small town in the Rocky Mountains, with her husband and three children. Both of them worked at blue-collar jobs in town. Even with both incomes, they just barely got by, and never had money for extra things. Diane found the opportunity she thought she was looking for... a low-cost investment. She looked into it, and liked what she learned. She could make this investment on her own, and proceeded to debate the issue. Though she wanted to give it a try, she just never felt the time was quite right. A year later, she still waited for the opportune time, and still hadn't made a decision. But, the opportunity had passed her by.

Have you ever observed couples while out to dinner? In many cases, neither one will make a decision on what they want to have. Each is determined to let the other make the first move, then follow suit. "What are you going to have?", he asks. "I don't know, what are you going to have?" she replies. "Well, I just can't make up my mind; why don't you pick?" he retorts. She responds "Oh, I just don't know what I want."

And, this goes on and on for minutes before finally one is forced into making a choice.

The boss was interviewing his new employee. "Would you say that you're decisive?" he asked. After a long pause, and a scratch of the chin, the employee slowly answered: "Well.... yes....and no.... you know.... maybe?"

Have you ever had a difficult time making a decision? Isn't it frustrating to not be able to make up our mind? We often don't understand or analyze this pattern of indecision and how it hurts our chances of succeeding? Our goal is to illuminate the trap of indecisiveness.

How Can I be Sure that I'm Indecisive?

This question itself may partially explain why we find it difficult to make decisions. One is seldom absolutely sure of anything in this imperfect world. Yet, sometimes we seek only the sure thing, that has no risk attached. However, since life is inherently risky, we never make a decision because we never find the perfect risk-free choice! If you relate to this, perhaps you should pause to reflect on the world in which you live. Can you identify even one significant choice that does not involve risk? Even selecting our meal while dining out with someone has risk. We might choose the same thing they wanted, or set a price range they find undesirable, or conflict with the wine they like. The point is that everything has risk! *If you're uncomfortable with even minimal **risk-taking**, it might explain why even mundane decisions are traumatic.*

There is a personality type often called "analytical," and many of us have this tendency. If you're a person who thrives on gathering information and facts, then analyzing them forwards and backwards before you'll make a decision, you might be holding yourself back. We, of course, want our important decisions to be based upon facts, not assumptions or opinions. The question is, how much factual information do we need? In every decision, there are <u>crucial considerations,</u>

and there are others which are <u>not critical</u>. Some information is simply trivial and not important to a specific decision. Once we have identified the crucial facts and factors, we have all the information we need to make a choice. If you find yourself always wanting to know more, like the example of Doug, *there is a point at which "analysis" becomes "indecision."*

We are frequently set up by society to develop into indecisive adults. Some of us may have a very domineering parent, who called all the shots, even into our adult years. We may have progressed through school systems which were very authoritarian, leaving little freedom to make our own decisions. Once we entered the working world, we could have supervisors and bosses with aggressive dominant personalities, who told us when to jump and how high. Perhaps our spouse has a very strong and forceful personality, and tends to have the last say on every subject. A person, experiencing years of such influences, can become meek and indecisive. This is not a rare situation, and many adults are negatively affected by years of subservience. *We can become conditioned to indecision if we're dependent upon others to make our decisions for us.*

For a variety of reasons, our confidence and self-esteem can erode to the point that we are unable to make choices and decisions. How is your self-confidence? Does it crush you to be wrong? The reality is that our decisions will occasionally be the wrong ones. If your ego and self-esteem are strong, you not only have the confidence to make choices, but you can live with the responsibility if they're wrong. On the other hand, *the person who has a low opinion of himself, and lacks confidence, will have a hard time making decisions.*

Indecision is often masked by excuses. It's easier to just say "I'm too busy," or "I don't have the time," than to make a demanding decision. Earlier, we looked at the underlying dishonesty in all excuses. When a person is afraid or lacks the self-esteem to make a decision, he doesn't want to admit that. So, usually he or she doesn't admit it, they just come up with a good-sounding excuse, which they hope will put the decision off indefinitely. For many of us, the hidden agenda behind our pet excuses is a fear or unwillingness to make decisions!

Some of us don't want to make decisions or excuses, so we just get preoccupied with other activities and ignore the issue altogether. Our example, Doug, used this tactic. Since he couldn't bring himself to make a decision, he became more entrenched in his sports habit. This tactic will work just fine, and has the same result as making an excuse: *nothing happens, and nothing changes!* Have you ever known someone who dealt with their hard choices by becoming wrapped up in something else, and ignoring it? If so, isn't indecision hurting their potential?

If any of these paragraphs seem to describe you, perhaps indecision is hindering your ability to get ahead in life. Neither you nor I can escape the avalanche of choices that life throws at our door. Unless we find the inner strength to face those choices head-on, not run from them, but instead develop the skill of making sound decisions, we will be forever on the defensive. And, **life will run us, we won't run life!**

What's the Big Deal, Anyway?

Andrew Carnegie, founder of U.S. Steel and many philanthropic activities, had strong beliefs about people. One belief he held was that any man (or woman), who had management and leadership qualities, should be able to make decisions quickly, once they knew the pertinent facts. He used to even time his employees with a stop watch, once he felt all the key facts were on the table. Unless his man could make a decision within one minute, that person was considered too indecisive and weak for higher responsibilities. *Carnegie knew that decision-making is simply a fact of life, and we had all better develop the ability....if we are going anywhere in life!*

Life is full of choices, and choices require decisions! Every single day of our lives, we are constantly making decisions, often without much conscious thought. Our choices can be as minor as choosing between breakfast cereals, or as major as making a career change. Either way, we still must come to some kind of decision, time and again throughout our waking hours. To attempt to avoid making decisions, is to attempt to avoid life! The only way you'll do so... is to die! So, we need to build our skill and habit of making decisions, or life will outrun us.

The little daily decisions of life may seem minor at the time, yet they add up to a major impact upon our lifetimes! Take one decision path in my life, for instance. Early in youth, I chose to be very interested in school. This led to good grades in high school, and subsequent acceptance into the University of Nebraska and the Air Force ROTC program, as a scholarship recipient. This led to completing the ROTC Flight Instruction Program, and to a slot in the Air Force Pilot Training school. Continued decisions along the flying career path, and on a civilian business path following retirement, led me to where I am today, writing these words. Had I made different choices my life would undoubtedly be drastically different. Every one of you is on a path directly resulting from the choices you have made to this time. Your future depends upon the quality of your decisions from now on!

You will make decisions, whether you want to or not!
Because even indecision is a "decision to change nothing"!
Do not misunderstand this point. Many people can not or will not make a decision, when confronted with choices. Often, they hum and haw for weeks on end, not willing to say "no," yet unable to say "yes." Eventually, the choice is made by default: no decision is a decision to stay on the path we're on. In many cases, it's apparent to the unbiased outside observer, that these people desperately need to consider other options. Despite their obvious needs, though, indecision keeps them on the same course, for better or worse.

Likewise, we occasionally trap ourselves with our analytical nature. We've already discussed the analytical personality, and their innate drive for information. If we allow ourselves to get hung up on an insatiable appetite for information, we will short-circuit our decision-making with trivia. I've heard this situation described as the ***"Paralysis of Analysis."*** *The end result is the same... no decision is ever reached, and no decision is a "decision to change nothing"!*

The big deal lies in the fact that indecision is a decision to change nothing. And, ***nothing changes until something changes!*** This is a natural law, which we often ignore. Many people need to do more than they're doing, for themselves and for their families, yet they're unwilling to make the decisions to change. A physical law says that an object does not change its present direction and speed until some force acts upon it. This law applies equally well to you and me. The present course we are on, whether we are satisfied with it or not, will not change until something or someone changes a governing factor. The inevitable circumstances of life will make changes for us, usually to our detriment, unless we take the bull by the horns and make the changes to get on a better path. *Nothing will change for the better for us, until we make a decision to make a change for the better!*

Indecision, for whatever reason, always has the same effect: it keeps us from improving our lives, because it makes us cling to the path we're on, even when we don't like the path!

OK, How do I Become more "Decisive"?

If you feel that indecision may be holding you back, you have already taken the first step to dealing with it. None of us can tackle a problem, until we recognize that we have it. Then, we need to convince ourselves that it is indeed a problem worth overcoming.

Stop and reflect upon the choices you've already made in life, whether by default or by intent. Haven't they determined where you are today? Doesn't it seem logical that future choices will effect where you end up years from now? If so, then it is of vital importance that you make your own decisions based upon facts and skill, not by defaulting them to someone else or to indecision. *Your future depends on it! If you have a family, their future depends on it as well!* You owe it to them, if not to yourself, to make sound and timely decisions.

Recognize that everything we do has an element of risk! You and I live in an imperfect world, and things don't always work out to our advantage. Do not allow yourself to become indecisive because you perceive some risk. The best you can ever hope for is to determine what the risks are, and to manage your decisions and your actions so as to keep the risks acceptable, when compared to the potential benefits. To expect more than this, is to be unrealistic!

Understand also that the <u>better</u> things in life almost always carry <u>greater</u> risks! If you invest, you already know that the best potential returns on your money come from the most risky investments. Life tends to be the same way. We cannot love, unless we accept the possibility of rejection and hurt. We cannot progress, without the chance of failure and discouragement. We cannot change ourselves for the better, and avoid criticism from those who don't understand. Plant this truth firmly in your mind: the succulent fruits are never nice and safe on the trunk of the tree; ***the fruit of life is always out on a limb!***

You must make the choice to become more decisive, or not! Like everything we discuss in this book, indecision stems from an attitude, and you and I have the option of controlling our attitude. We chose to become indecisive, and we'll choose if we stay that way. We also have the choice to become decisive. There is no excuse, and there is no one else to pin the blame on, the decision is **ours**! If you decide to break the back of indecision in your life, you are halfway to success!

Any tool you use, to help you logically evaluate your choices and arrive at a sound decision, is a potential asset. Some techniques are as simple as writing out all the important pros and cons, then crossing them off against offsetting items, until you have an imbalance on either the pro or the con side. Others might have you compare the probable risks with the anticipated rewards, and determine whether the risk is acceptable in light of what you stand to gain. For more complicated and major decisions, a decision matrix may be helpful. Whatever tool you might use, the ultimate decision will still be <u>your best judgment</u> based upon the factors you've considered. Decision tools are still tools, and can never guarantee the best decision. They are better than using nothing, and, over a lifetime of use, will assuredly result in more good decisions than poor ones!

All that remains is to develop the ability and skill for making sound, intelligent, logical decisions. To this end, there are many excellent resources and decision-making tools. *Self-improvement resources will not only teach you better thought habits and decision-making techniques, but can help you increase your self-esteem and confidence, thereby freeing you to trust more in your ability to make good choices.*

Finding the courage and determination to make wise decisions, whenever you need to make them, can only help you... it will not hurt you. Indecision, on the other hand, will keep you from reaching the real fruit of life!

Making decisions is part of the battle... but it's only half the battle! The other half is sticking to the decisions that we make!

CHAPTER TWENTY-FOUR
AT THE END OF YOUR ROPE? ..... GOOD!

I stood in my fourth floor German apartment, at the open window. I had only been in Germany for two months, and had no close friends or family there to lean on for support. My Air Force duty was extremely demanding, and I was under a great deal of professional stress. For several weeks, I had rested less than two hours daily with very troubled and broken sleep. The work, though, wasn't the problem. In my hand, I held the paperwork to bring my wife, four-year-old daughter, and thirteen-year-old stepdaughter to Germany from the United States. I had expected them to accompany me on this assignment, once I found suitable housing. In my mind, I replayed the phone call over and over, and the words which literally brought me to my knees: "I'm not coming. I want a divorce." The pain I felt was unbearable! I looked at the ground, forty feet below, and debated if life was worth living. I felt like a total loser!

Many of us feel trapped in failure sometimes! For some of us, this sense of hopelessness and frustration may be the result of a bad marriage relationship. For others, it could come from financial crisis, usually the product of one or more bad decisions, and combined with an inadequate income. Another person may have an addiction to alcohol, drugs, or something else, which consumes their waking hours and dominates their thoughts. *And, for many of us, this dull ache in our hearts may just be the product of sheer mediocrity... lives of insignificance, going nowhere!* Nothing really terrible, yet few things that are deeply satisfying, drifting through the years, with little changing, except our age. This too, can be an extremely frustrating feeling, and can also leave us feeling... *at the end of our rope!*

If this relates to you or to a person you know, and there is a growing sense of frustration, hopelessness, and maybe even bitterness at the bad hand life has dealt, don't despair! We can look at this from two opposite perspectives. From the negative perspective, we have been "done wrong," and now have the right to a major pity-party, complaining, whining, crying, and pointing the blame at everyone and everything else. Everyone would totally understand if we just rolled over, tucked our tail, and gave up, as I considered doing. *Or, we can see this from a positive point of view: Life is trying to tell us... we need to do something different!*

What It Means When In Crisis?

We all experience crises from time to time. Sooner or later, death, illness, injury, bad financial choices, and failing relationships seem to affect us all. These bad times never come at a good time for any of us, and they may come in many different forms, for a great variety of reasons, and may mean different things to each of us. However, periods of great distress, anguish, pain, frustration, and hopelessness, all have one thing in common. *When you and I are at our lowest, when life seems unworthy of even living, when everything has gone sour on us, and when there seems to be no way out of the quagmire we find ourselves in, life is telling us...*
...It's time for us to change!

Most people have a natural resistance to change! We all tend to get used to doing things a certain way, to eating the same types of foods, to thinking, talking and acting in a similar manner. Some of us squeeze the toothpaste tube from the bottom up, others from the top down. Others want the toilet paper to roll out from the top, while another may expect it from the back and bottom. We become comfortable with a pattern of behavior that we're familiar with, no matter what it is or how productive it is for us. The same is true of our occupations, our hobbies, our friendships, and our associations. We don't want to change, because change takes us out of our comfort zone and requires extra effort and a degree of uncertainty. While the things we are doing may not be doing much for us, at least they are familiar and predictable. They become habit, and habits are hard to break.

When the sum total of our habits brings us to the brink of disaster and we hit bottom, from the pit of despair comes at least one potential benefit. *We may now acknowledge the need for change, and finally be willing to make changes which can improve ourselves and our lives! History proves time and again, that when one reaches this point... great things are possible!*

Failure and Success Have This In Common!

"Rome wasn't built in a day!" Have you ever heard this timeless quote? It's telling us the common sense wisdom that major events, and situations, don't usually happen overnight. They are the natural result of days, weeks, months, and years of decisions, indecision, actions, inaction, attention, neglect, good choices and wrong choices which lead inevitably to the present circumstances. This is almost invariably true of our failures, and of our successes!

Failure, at anything of significance, occurs in the same way that Rome was built: one brick and board at a time! Look deeply into any of your perceived failures, and analyze the process by which they became a failure. In most cases, you'll find a pattern of wrong choices, neglect, and improper actions spanning many months, or even years. A marriage doesn't usually fall into divorce court overnight for one catastrophic reason. Usually, it has been coming apart slowly over a considerable period of time, one neglected need, one forgotten birthday, one misunderstanding, at a time. Day after day, the little things do add up and do mean a lot!

Success, at anything of significance, has the same common thread. It also occurs in daily habits, in everyday thoughts and actions, day upon day, month after month, year following year. I've heard success described as a journey or a process, rather than an event, for this reason. *It takes place one stone, one brick, one word, one right thought, one right decision, one proper deed...* **one success habit at a time, for as long as it takes!**

Failure and success also have this in common: life happens! The path to both is strewn with rocks and holes, stumbling blocks, circumstances beyond our control, which can profoundly affect our journey. The road to success, just as that to failure, will seldom be smooth, straight, and level. It will always be rutted with interruptions, twist and curve with unanticipated challenges, and have steep uphill grades with unwanted barriers and distractions which slow us down. *If we're to succeed at anything worthwhile, we must simply expect to be challenged and tested, and we must expect to pay the price in persistence and determination!*

Mount Rushmore, in the Black Hills near Rapid City, South Dakota, is one example of the journey toward success. Commissioned as a national monument in 1925, after a difficult process of building influential support for such a grand undertaking, work was begun in 1927. It was not completed until 1941. During construction, there were planning, weather, political, safety, and technological challenges. Plans had to be changed several years into the project, necessitating the move of a face to a different position on the mountain. Critics and skeptics were in plentiful supply, and some felt this was not only an impossible task but a colossal waste of money and resources. Sculptor and artist, Gutzon Borglum, died prior to completion, and his son, Lincoln, had to finish what his father had started. Despite all obstacles, Mount Rushmore stands today as not just a national monument to four presidents and to freedom, but a monument to the power of determination and persistence!

Positive change, and the journey to success, are like a ladder: we start at the bottom rung, and go forward and upward... one step, a second, the third, fourth... as long as it takes, until we get to the top!

Do It Now!

Have you ever taken a vacation? If so, did you feel the timing was perfect, your work was caught up, the loose ends were completely tied up, everyone was totally ready, and the entire situation was under control? Unless you're very exceptional, you're probably like the rest of us, and have not experienced this state of vacation utopia. The reality for most is, if we have a typically busy life, we rarely if ever have a perfect time to get away. It usually comes down to just going... or not going. The same is true with making positive changes in ourselves!

When changes are necessary, in ourselves or our conditions, the timing will almost never be convenient, nor will the situation be what we want it to be! In fact, the entire circumstances will probably be quite inconvenient and unfavorable, otherwise, change is likely not needed. So, if we have reached the end of our rope, and we know that something simply has to change, then you and I must accept that the situation won't be perfect and the timing won't be right. *If we expect perfection before we begin to make appropriate changes, we'll never make the changes!*

Likewise, our past is irrelevant, with regard to whether we should or can effect change for the better. Past history is just that... past history! There is absolutely nothing we can do to change what has taken place. We can only influence what we do now, and where it will lead in the future. Our past can only be used in one of two ways. In the negative way, we can dwell on the past and fret, worry, and despair over the things that have taken place; the water that has gone under the bridge; what we should have said or not said; what we should have done or not done. Such an attitude only costs us time, sleep, health, and forward progress! Or, we may look at our past in the positive light. *We can look backward only for the learning value, the lessons taught, and we can then go forward, more wisely!*

It may sound trite, and over-used, but nevertheless it is still true, "today is the first day of the rest of your life"! You and I may come up with every reason and excuse in the book for why we can't change, why our situation is different. Yet, change is still necessary. And, it doesn't alter the fact that our lives are only going to be so long, and we don't know how long that is. Every day we delay is just one less day we'll have. One less day to positively effect our situation and habits. One less day to make a difference, and benefit from it. *There's no time like the present... **do it now!***

If you know you need to change... why not get started! What will you gain by waiting?

What Is Your Potential?

Do you know what your full potential is? Just what are you capable of doing and becoming? How far can you go in life? Do you have a good idea? Some idea? No idea? In all likelihood, most of us have very little notion of our true potential as a human being. As a result, with few exceptions, we sell ourselves short and we accomplish far less than we are capable of.

One may look across the smooth surface of a lake, and see an expanse of water. But, what lies beneath the surface? Some lakes hide untold secrets, perhaps ancient skeletons, wrecked boats, in some cases even entire towns lie submerged. Larger lakes may harbor fish of staggering size, and some notoriously famous "monsters" allegedly swim the murky depths of one or two bodies of water. Yet, who would suspect what lies beneath the surface, hidden from view to the casual observer? You are like these lakes, and your surface exterior conceals unknown and unexplored treasures, undiscovered abilities, unreached destiny! Only by purposely looking inside, exploring within, and challenging this unused territory, can we begin to understand and ascertain the full measure of our capability.

In 1880, a girl named Helen Adams Keller was born in Alabama. As an infant, a tragic illness left her blind, deaf, and unable to speak. Trapped in a world without sound, sight, nor communication, Helen Keller was destined to be little more than a human vegetable, totally dependent upon someone else for her very existence. However, a compassionate and very determined woman came into little seven-year-old Helen's life. Anne Sullivan, from the Perkins Institute for the Blind, was not willing to doom Helen Keller to a life of nothingness.

Through sheer force of will, and the power of persistence, Anne Sullivan taught Helen to "hear" through touch, and then to communicate the same way. With this opening of her world, Helen learned to "see" the world through the communication of others. She went on to write her first published work at the age of 23, the first of seven books. Helen Keller lives on in history as a source of inspiration, courage, determination, and a testimony to friendship that doesn't accept limits. All this, because one person had the vision to help a little girl find her full potential! Can your potential be any less than Helen Keller's?

Og Mandino was a World War II Army Air Corps bombardier, flying thirty combat missions with Jimmy Stewart's group. Following the war, he failed at a brief attempt to become a writer, then found work with an insurance company. However, poor training, persistent debt, and the stress of his work eventually led him to alcoholism, depression, and a good-bye note from his wife and daughter. Self-pity and alcohol became his way of life, as he drifted from city to city. He sank deeper into despair, until one cold, damp day he found himself contemplating suicide. In his own words, he "didn't have the guts" to even end his life, and he instead wandered into a library for warmth. Seeking comfort in reading, a habit he once loved, he picked up a self-help book.

In *Success Through a Positive Mental Attitude*, Og found the messages which helped him change his life. He began to regain self-control, get his pride back, and shed the bonds of alcohol. Soon he had remarried. Then, he accepted an opportunity to become Executive Editor for *Success Unlimited*, a motivational periodical for business and sales people. Thus began a phenomenal writing career. Until his death in 1996, Og Mandino wrote more than a dozen books, and became one of the world's best known motivational and inspirational success authors and speakers. Millions of people are better off because Og Mandino lived, and because he changed the circumstances of his life, to reach for his greatest potential! This story comes from one of his own bestsellers, *A Better Way to Live*, written in 1990.

How big are your challenges? If Helen Keller and Og Mandino could reach the heights they did... how far might you go? What's your potential? What's keeping you from finding it?

At the Fork in the Road

In Germany, I found myself at a fork in the road of my life. Going straight ahead, on the path I had been on, was no longer an option. I could only go to the left, or to the right, and either way involved change. My "apple-cart" had been upset. I now had to either salvage what I could and go on with what remained; or, I could lie down, wallow in self-pity, and give up. Struggling to find the strength to go on, several sayings would come into my mind, over and over again. Only now do I realize how important they were to me during that period of dark depression!

It's always darkest before the dawn! Behind every cloud is a silver lining! I have a daughter who needs me! I must find a way... for her sake!

It was not easy! Believing that life simply had to be better one day meant living with the pain and frustration at the moment. A lot of moments! But, I held on, and slowly moved forward, one step, one tear, one heartache, one small victory at a time.

Recently, I returned from visiting my now adult daughter, a lovely and loving young woman. I played basketball, and dreamed about the future, with my son-in-law. I read and took walks with my two-year-old grandson. I held my tiny new granddaughter.

It was worth the struggle! It was worth enduring the pain! It was worth embracing the changes!

Are you at a fork in your road? Is the path you were on no longer an option? If so, embrace the change. Your life can only get worse... or better. If it must change anyway, and it's your choice, why not start making changes for the better? Why not start today?

Each dawn... brings a new day!

You're only a loser if you give up, quit, accept mediocrity.

As long as you're genuinely trying, still in the fight, refusing defeat, rejecting mediocrity...

... *You're a winner!*

BIBLIOGRAPHY
of
Recommended Books, Resources, and References.

1. Allen, James. *As A Man Thinketh*. Grossett & Dunlap. New York, NY.

2. Carnegie, Dale. 1944. *How To Stop Worrying and Start Living*. Simon & Schuster, Inc. New York, NY.

3. Carnegie, Dale, & Associates. 1993. *The Leader In You*. Simon & Schuster, Inc. New York, NY.

4. Cole, Edwin Louis. 1982. *Maximized Manhood*. Whitaker House. Springdale, PA.

5. Conwell, Russell H. 1960. *Acres of Diamonds*. Fleming H. Revell Company. Old Tappan, NJ.

6. Cooper, Darien B. 1974. *You Can Be the Wife of a Happy Husband*. Victor Books. Wheaton, IL.

7. DeVos, Richard M., with Charles Paul Conn. 1975. *Believe*. The Berkley Publishing Group. New York, NY.

8. Getty, J. Paul. 1965. *How to be Rich*. The Berkley Publishing Group. New York, NY.

9. Giblin, Les. 1956. *How to Have Confidence and Power in Dealing with People*. Prentice-Hall, Inc. Englewood Cliffs, NJ.

10. Hedges, Burke. 1995. *You Can't Steal Second with Your Foot on First*. INTI Publishing. Tampa, FL.

11. Hill, Napoleon. 1960. *Success Through a Positive Mental Attitude*. Simon & Schuster, Inc. New York, NY.

12. Hill, Napoleon. 1965. *The Master Key to Riches*. Ballantine Books. New York, NY.

13. Kreidman, Ellen. 1991. *Light His Fire* and *Light Her Fire* (audio tapes). LHF Enterprises. El Toro, CA.

14. Mandino, Og. 1984. *The Choice*. Bantam Books. New York, NY.

15. Mandino, Og. 1975. *The Greatest Miracle in the World*. Bantam Books. New York, NY.

16. Mandino, Og. 1982. *University of Success*. Bantam Books. New York, NY.

17. Marden, Orison Swett. 1910. *The Miracle of Right Thought*. Sun Publishing Company. Sante Fe, NM.

18. Matthews, Andrew. 1990. *Being Happy*. Price Stern Sloan, Inc. Los Angeles, CA.

19. Peale, Norman Vincent. 1964. *Enthusiasm Makes the Difference*. Ballantine Books. New York, NY.

20. Schwartz, David J. 1959. *The Magic of Thinking Big*. Simon & Schuster, Inc. New York, NY.

21. Smalley, Gary. 1979. *For Better Or For Best*. Harper Paper Backs. New York, NY.

22. Smalley, Gary. 1979. *If Only He Knew*. Harper Paper Backs. New York, NY.

23. Smalley, Gary. 1993. *Hidden Keys to Loving Relationships* (video tapes). Gary Smalley Seminars, Inc.

ABOUT THE AUTHOR

Bernard H. (Bernie) Burgess is a retired United States Air Force officer and pilot. He presently lives in Cody, Wyoming with his wife, Olivia, where they own and operate a bed and breakfast, and are involved in various other enterprises. He also teaches the same subjects he has written about in this book, through a workshop he calls "Success Concepts."

Bernie was born in Alliance, Nebraska in 1947, the oldest of four children, to Sandhill ranchers, Bernard and Ruth Burgess. He grew up as his parents "right-hand man." At the age of eight, he was helping with ranch work and chores, and driving himself to a one-room country school in the "little Jeep." Frequently he rode to school on one of their many horses, three-and-a-half miles each way. His family did not have electric power, an indoor bathroom, nor a television until he was nearly a teenager, and he remembers very well the old "two-holer" out south of the house. Because of the distance and lack of telephone service, Bernie boarded out in town his first two years of high school. Despite this lack of modern amenities, he would be quick to tell you that his childhood was great, filled with love, caring, and working side-by-side with his parents and siblings in the outdoors work of cattleranching.

In high school, Bernie was active in every available sport and student government function. Graduating as a co-valedictorian, he then attended the University of Nebraska at Lincoln, Nebraska. In college, he worked part-time all four years and received several scholarships, including an Air Force Reserve Officers Training Corps scholarship. His interest in the Air Force resulted in graduating as a Distinguised Graduate of the ROTC program and entering the Air Force as an officer and pilot.

An Air Force career led him to such varied places as Washington, DC; Little Rock, Arkansas; Kaiserslautern, Germany; Abilene, Texas; Tokyo, Japan; and central New Jersey. As a pilot, he flew in Central America, the Caribbean, Europe, the Mediterranean, Africa, and the Western Pacific regions, as well as North America. He performed duties as an instructor and evaluator pilot, as a command and control officer managing airlift operations, and as a manager and leader of people. He retired from active duty in 1990.

Since retirement from the military, Bernie has followed his dreams of living in the Northwest United States, being in business, and making a difference.